GOD'S WONDER WOMEN (PART 1)

BY

CATHERINE BROWN

Published by
GGM Publishing
../AppData/Local/Microsoft/Windows/Temporary Internet
Files/Content.IE5/X3CZWUM6/www.TransparentPublishing
.co.uk
©GGM Publishing

Original Copyright holder - Catherine Brown

Unless otherwise indicated, Biblical quotations are from the
old King James Version of the bible. Public Domain

GGM Publishing, 18 Castleview, West Kilbride, Ayrshire,
KA23 9HD, Scotland, UK

CONTENTS

INTRODUCTION

JESUS AND WOMEN

Wonder Woman – Who is She?

In 2017 I was fascinated by observing the responses of women old and young, Christian and non-Christian, as they watched the Hollywood blockbuster movie *Wonder Woman*. I watched it myself with my daughter and arrived at the conclusion that the Hollywood producers captured something that I believe the church is slow to realise – they understand that women can be heroes too *and* that women need role models from amongst women.

In March 2018 I had the privilege of ministering in Sydney, Australia. I was with some young Aboriginal women at one of the meetings and I asked them who their role models were today. Many of them answered, "Wonder Woman," citing the fictional movie character as a personal inspiration to them. Here she was again influencing an emerging generation!

A woman can be beautiful, intelligent, compassionate, strong and capable of influencing the destiny of nations. A woman can be merciful and a warrior at the same time. She can be compassionate and yet still be strategic.

This book is in part a response to the worldwide phenomenon of the restoration of women in society and in church. It is not intended to be an apologetic per se. In the global trend of #MeToo it is a time for truth and restoration. My intention in this first volume of *God's Wonder Women* is simply to celebrate remarkable women from a Kingdom perspective by revisiting the narrative of some women in Scripture through the lens of their life stories.

Jesus Championed Women

Women have always played a significant role in the Kingdom of God and in the ministry of Jesus Christ Himself.

In the Old Testament we meet heroines of the faith such as Sarah who conceived in her old age and through her children blessed the nations with the twelve tribes of Israel; Queen Esther who saved a nation, Deborah the Prophetess, Judge and Military leader who became a deliverer of a nation; Ruth the Moabite who became the wife of Boaz and continued the lineage of Christ; Leah the once rejected wife of Jacob, who became a much loved matriarch and together with her sister Rachel build up the house of Israel; In their lives we see clear paradigms of capable, anointed women entrusted with positions of power, influence and authority under the grace of God.

As we move on into the New Testament era we cannot fail to observe how Jesus' ministry was supported by women from all walks of life and in a variety of ways. Women were His disciples. They were amongst the first who served Christ and who were also discipled by Him.

Jesus championed women young and the old, rich and poor, the rejected and discarded of society as well as those with influence and power. Just a brief glance at the Gospel narratives, reveal that He reinstated women post-Eden to a more glorious condition because of the finished work of Calvary.

Women in ministry leadership positions continued after the Lord's ascension, include such women as Phoebe, Junias the wife of Andronicus (both the husband and wife regarded as apostles by Apostle Paul); Philip's daughters were recognised as prophetess'; Lois the grandmother of Timothy and his mother were both acknowledged by Apostle Paul in their roles as bringing up Timothy in the faith to be a great man of God. The bible is full of examples of women whom God championed as His ambassadors in many spheres of society and church life. Women emerge as history makers, culture shapers and thought leaders.

Jesus' ministry would not have been possible without His mother Mary. The angel Gabriel's words to the young Mary, *37 For with God nothing shall be impossible* are responded to by her in a miraculous and courageous way, as the young woman whom God had set aside to become the Virgin mother of our Lord and Saviour Jesus Christ. Mary's immediate faith-filled answer is an inspiration to us still today. *38 And Mary said, Behold the handmaid of the Lord; be it unto me according to thy word. And the angel departed from her. Luke 1*

At His birth Anna the Prophetess prophesied concerning Jesus' destiny. She was 84 years old but whilst elderly in human age terms, she was powerfully used by God at a critical time in the history of the nations,
38 And she coming in that instant gave thanks likewise unto the Lord, and spake of him to all them that looked for redemption in Jerusalem.
Luke 2

At His first miracle during the wedding at Cana, Mary His mother was instrumental in setting things in motion. *5 His mother saith unto the servants, Whatsoever he saith unto you, do it" John 2:5* remains one of the wisest statements anyone has ever said concerning response to Christ's instructions!

Women Disciples

Throughout His ministry Jesus was often surrounded by women who were an integral and essential part of His ministry. Such women include Mary Magdalene, Joanna the wife of Cuza (the manager of Herod's household); Susanna and many others. Scripture records these women served Him in various capacities including financially undergirding the ministry of Jesus Christ. These women were helping to support Jesus and His ministry out of their own means.

Importantly the context of their being with Christ is set *first of all in their roles in discipleship* – verse 1 of Luke 8 records the Twelve as being the Lord and involved in Kingdom ministry. Verse 2 immediately follows on to say that certain women were also part of that company. The implication, therefore, is that the women were involved in Kingdom ministry also along with the men.

8 And it came to pass afterward, that he went throughout every city and village, preaching and shewing the glad tidings of the kingdom of God: and the twelve were with him, 2 And certain women, which had been healed of evil spirits and infirmities, Mary called Magdalene, out of whom went seven devils, 3 And Joanna the wife of Chuza Herod's steward, and Susanna, and many others, which ministered unto him of their substance. Luke 8

In Jesus' final moments on the Cross Mary His mother, and his mother's sister, Mary the wife of Cleophas and Mary Magdalene were all present along with John the beloved. *27 Then saith he to the disciple, Behold thy mother! And from that hour that disciple took her unto his own home. John 19*

At His resurrection Jesus appeared to Mary Magdalene and sent her as a witness of His resurrection. It is fair to say this is the most important piece of information that could ever have been carried by any messenger in any nation in any period of human history and Jesus entrusted this same message to a woman! *17 Jesus saith unto her, Touch me not; for I am not yet ascended to my Father: but go to my brethren, and say unto them, I ascend unto my Father, and your Father; and to my God, and your God. John 20*

Not only are women featured prominently in the ministry of Jesus Christ and the New Testament Church, they are also used by the Lord to teach us essential doctrinal principles such as the resurrection from the dead, worship, giving, demonstration of healing and much more.

Resurrection Miracles

Jesus raised the 12-year old daughter of Jairus from the dead, demonstrating His power over life and death even before He had gone to the Cross. *39 And when he was come in, he saith unto them, Why make ye this ado, and weep? the damsel is not dead, but sleepeth. 40 And they laughed him to scorn. But when he had put them all out, he taketh the father and the mother of the damsel, and them that were with him, and entereth in where the damsel was lying. 41 And he took the damsel by the hand, and said unto her, Talitha cumi; which is, being interpreted, Damsel, I say unto thee, arise. 42 And straightway the damsel arose, and walked; for she was of the age of twelve years. And they were astonished with a great astonishment. Mark 5*

In the community of Nain Jesus raised the widow's only son back to life leaving His disciples and the surrounding regions in no doubt of His resurrection power. *13 And when the Lord saw her, he had compassion on her, and said unto her, Weep not. 14 And he came and touched the bier: and they that bare him stood still. And he said, Young man, I say unto thee, Arise. 15 And he that was dead sat up, and began to speak. And he delivered him to his mother. Luke 7*

Teaching on Giving

Jesus used the seemingly insignificant offering of a widow woman to mark the history books and our hearts with the poignant truth of giving: it is not the amount given but the heart and sacrificial love behind giving that make the difference to God and in our lives. *41 And Jesus sat over against the treasury, and beheld how the people cast money into the treasury: and many that were rich cast in much. 42 And there came a certain poor widow, and she threw in two mites, which make a farthing. 43 And he called unto him his disciples, and saith unto them, Verily I say unto you, That this poor widow hath cast more in, than all they which have cast into the treasury: 44 For all they did cast in of their abundance; but she of her want did cast in all that she had, even all her living. Mark 12*

Teaching on Worship

Luke shares with us the poignant story of a sinful woman, most probably a prostitute, who somehow found her way to the feet of Jesus whilst He was having supper at the home of Simon the Pharisee. She was reviled by all, her tarnished reputation preceding her. Yet the Lord did not reject her and in fact, used her to reveal to us the true heart of humility and genuine worship. She found acceptance in the presence of Jesus, while Simon the Pharisee is revealed for the two-faced hypocrite that he truly was. *47 Wherefore I say unto thee, Her sins, which are many, are forgiven; for she loved much: but to whom little is forgiven, the same loveth little. Luke 7*

Demonstrating Healing

There are numerous instances of Jesus healing both men, women and children. But for now let me reference two example. The woman who bled for twelve years was healed as she touched the hem of Jesus. She demonstrated incredible faith and courage to reach out to Him in the condition of being "unclean" because of her bleeding. Her faith was rewarded and she was received as a daughter by the

Lord Himself, *22 But Jesus turned him about, and when he saw her, he said, Daughter, be of good comfort; thy faith hath made thee whole. And the woman was made whole from that hour. Matthew 9*

Another example of overcoming dire circumstance is given us in the woman who had been crippled for eighteen years who was healed by the Lord Jesus in the synagogue on the Sabbath. Despite her many years of suffering she was found in church listening to the power of the word being preached by Jesus. God was faithful to her and changed the destiny of not only one woman but also an entire community through her healing testimony. *12 And when Jesus saw her, he called her to him, and said unto her, Woman, thou art loosed from thine infirmity.13 And he laid his hands on her: and immediately she was made straight, and glorified God. Luke 13*

Teaching on Prayer

The Lord used the example of a persistent widow to teach His disciples concerning the principle of prevailing prayer and that sometimes we must learn to pray to Him in a judicial capacity. *18 And he spake a parable unto them to this end, that men ought always to pray, and not to faint; verse 1*

This little book *God's Wonder Women* is a celebration of women in an all walks of society whether they are in faith, science, medicine, arts, music, media, education, politics, government and any other sphere of society. As mothers, wives, sisters, aunts, grandmothers, friends, daughters, nieces, cousins I want to say thank you to every incredible woman I know! Keep soaring and don't stop till you fulfil your dreams in Jesus' mighty name. You were made to make a difference. You were created for the glory of God for great and mighty exploits. You are an ambassador of Heaven and an expression of the heart of our Heavenly Father! God bless you as you continue in your walk with Christ in whatever capacity He has called you.

CHAPTER 1 – DESTINY HELPERS

8 Now there arose up a new king over Egypt, which knew not Joseph. 9 And he said unto his people, Behold, the people of the children of Israel are more and mightier than we: 10 Come on, let us deal wisely with them; lest they multiply, and it come to pass, that, when there falleth out any war, they join also unto our enemies, and fight against us, and so get them up out of the land. 11 Therefore they did set over them taskmasters to afflict them with their burdens. And they built for Pharaoh treasure cities, Pithom and Raamses. 12 But the more they afflicted them, the more they multiplied and grew. And they were grieved because of the children of Israel. 13 And the Egyptians made the children of Israel to serve with rigour: 14 And they made their lives bitter with hard bondage, in morter, and in brick, and in all manner of service in the field: all their service, wherein they made them serve, was with rigour.
Exodus 1

Long gone were the glory days of Joseph's rule in Egypt, with the Hebrew people fallen into desperately hard times. A new Pharaoh had risen to power in Egypt, one who was afraid of the power and influence of the Hebrew people and who had chosen to deal with them cruelly and oppressively. The people of God were afflicted and endured great pain and suffering. Yet, despite the evil king's best efforts God's people continued to multiply and their number grew exponentially. In a last ditch attempt to destroy the Hebrew people the king made a decree that all baby boys born to Hebrew women were to be destroyed by the Hebrew midwives. The destiny of the nation of God hung in the balance. It is into such a context that we will discover how God raised up five groups of female *Destiny Helpers*:

1. Midwives
2. Mum
3. Sister
4. Maids
5. Daughter of Pharaoh

They were a diverse social strata group of cross-cultural women who became destiny helpers to Moses. God revealed through their lives and actions how He can and will use women from all positions and none at all, from humble backgrounds to royalty, from the professional world to family members from modest households to fulfil His purposes and plans in our lives, to reverse the plans of any enemy and to redeem our lives for His great glory and good. We will discover that we all need destiny helpers, and by the grace of God each one of us also has the capacity to become a destiny helper to others.

The Midwives – God-Fearing Women in Action

15 And the king of Egypt spake to the Hebrew midwives, of which the name of the one was Shiphrah, and the name of the other Puah: 16 And he said, When ye do the office of a midwife to the Hebrew women, and see them upon the stools; if it be a son, then ye shall kill him: but if it be a daughter, then she shall live.17 But the midwives feared God, and did not as the king of Egypt commanded them, but saved the men children alive.18 And the king of Egypt called for the midwives, and said unto them, Why have ye done this thing, and have saved the men children alive?19 And the midwives said unto Pharaoh, Because the Hebrew women are not as the Egyptian women; for they are lively, and are delivered ere the midwives come in unto them.20 Therefore God dealt well with the midwives: and the people multiplied, and waxed very mighty.21 And it came to pass, because the midwives feared God, that he made them houses.22 And Pharaoh charged all his people, saying, Every son that is born ye shall cast into the river, and every daughter ye shall save alive.

The midwives were surely part of a company of other female midwives but on this occasion the Bible gives us the names of only two of these amazing women: *Shiprah* meaning 'beautiful' and *Puah,* meaning 'splendid' or 'to cry out.'

The midwives were the first of the destiny helpers we encounter in the pre-birth and early life of Moses. They are described as God-fearing women, who were extremely smart, discerning, fast on their feet and merciful; in short - a tremendous example of faith in action. They had the capacity to think strategically. They were heroic, tenacious and wise and were uniquely positioned to be destiny helpers to Moses by dint of both their faith and their profession i.e. they were trained midwives. God used these midwives some time before Moses was even born. We see in this how God will always make preparations behind the scenes as well as being ever present with us in times of turmoil.

Pharaoh's edict meant that the midwives had been instructed to kill any baby boy children born to the Hebrew women. Despite this the midwives were God-fearing and they did not obey the king and instead allowed the male children to live. We cannot underestimate their courageous stance. Women have courage and when we take a stand for what we believe in things change, especially when we stand together in unity with God's will!

After some time had passed the king discovered that the midwives had disobeyed him and summoned them into his presence to ask them why they had done this thing and had not killed the Hebrew baby boys. He was in a position to destroy them yet they did not cow tow to intimidation. Their fear of God had lifted them above any fear of man and they made a choice to be women who preserved life rather than destroy it. They refused to allow themselves to be bullied. Word!

It is remarkable to witness the favour they experienced before the king whom they were actively disobeying and we must surely attribute this to the grace of God multiplied upon their lives through their obedience to God and their hearts of humility and love. God is still looking for women (and men) who will do likewise when all others are losing their heads. God needs those who can stand for what is right and righteous by His standards in times of adversity and moral decay and depravity.

The midwives were quick witted and responded with an extremely clever answer to the king's question, stating that the reason they couldn't obey him was because of the speed at which the Hebrew women gave birth, *"for they are lively, and are delivered ere the midwives come in unto them."*

The next two Scripture verses are a wonderful confirmation of God acting on behalf of His people and the reward that our obedience releases from Heaven to earth. Verse 20 states that God dealt well with the midwives and as a result of their faith in action, the people increased greatly in numbers thus routing the plans of the enemy (at least temporarily).

Verse 21 records that because the midwives had feared God, *"that he made them houses."* The two midwives received houses from Pharaoh by the will of God. The narrative states it is 'houses' i.e. it is a plural description. This gift was a multiple reward not a single house! Wow! For their obedience to God and standing for righteousness in a time of personal danger they were blessed beyond measure, both spiritually and physically. Surely this is an encouragement to our faith today.

Jesus Himself championed a similar message of reward and obedience in a discourse with His disciples, *29 And every one that hath forsaken houses, or brethren, or sisters, or father, or mother, or wife, or children, or lands, for my name's sake, shall receive an hundredfold, and shall inherit everlasting life.30 But many that are first shall be last; and the last shall be first Matthew 19*

Eventually the king realised that the midwives had outsmarted him and that he would need to do something else. In a sinister development he released a total death edict in the nation stating that *"every son that is born ye shall cast into the river, and every daughter ye shall save alive."* Never was there a more serious time for a boy child to be born, yet it is into this exact scenario that Moses was about to be delivered.

The Mother (Jochebed)

²And there went a man of the house of Levi, and took to wife a daughter of Levi. ² And the woman conceived, and bare a son: and when she saw him that he was a goodly child, she hid him three months.

Moses' mother was unique amongst women! She is our example of the quiet and tenacious faith of a mother. I want us to give some thought to her situation. It is likely that she gave birth to Moses alone, without the aid of a midwife. Given the aforementioned lethal edict of the king, it is logical to assume that Hebrew women would have given birth away from the public gaze and in relative solitude to protect the life of their unborn child.

Personally, I have given birth to four children and I am so grateful for the doctors, midwives and medical people who were on hand to assist. My third child was delivered by emergency caesarean and it was necessary to have medical intervention. I can only marvel at Moses' mother who most likely gave birth alone, without any kind of pain killers, and without another soul or a midwife by her side yet even in her solitude God was with her. He could never abandon such a precious woman of God, birthing such a son of destiny! I want to say to you now that you are not alone. God is with you!

I encourage us to reflect on those early days that she had with her new born baby for she only had three months with her little one before she had to make a life or death decision. During that time I marvel at how she must have prayed day by day, crying out to God, "I don't know how you will do it Lord, but I trust you. I don't know what to do Lord, but I ask you for answers. I don't know who to turn to Lord, but I know you are faithful." Like Moses' mother I'm sure most of us can empathise for there are times in life when we have the same things or prayed the same prayer, albeit for different reasons.

The Father

Imagine the father of Moses also, and perhaps even the older sister who we will hear more of shortly. This father is not named but we thank God for a man who loved his family and desired to protect them and provide for them. Like his wife, he also had to trust in God's mercy and overarching care. I'm sure he was a great and loving dad who also feared and loved God and did all he could for his family.

A family knowing the time with their little one was so precious and limited, would have prayed with all the power available to them from Heaven. I want us to immerse ourselves in what it meant for that family to pray for the destiny of their new-born child. This mother was a prayer warrior for a son of destiny who faced the most awful and impossible of circumstances. Let her example inspire us to pray more diligently and fervently for our own children and those who are entrusted to our care.

Like Mary the mother of Christ, Moses' mum took up a position of resolute faith. She nursed her child not knowing what the future would hold, but trusting the One who held their future. Like Mary, I am certain Moses' mother had a heart that believed nothing was impossible for God. But let us not be flippant concerning the treachery of the days in which she lived, nor miss the enormity of her faith and commitment to the Lord despite horrendous circumstances. She rises resplendent as a mother of faith. Her example becomes our precedent and our pattern as women of faith entrusted with sons and daughters of destiny.

The Revelation of the Basket

3And when she could not longer hide him, she took for him an ark of bulrushes, and daubed it with slime and with pitch, and put the child therein; and she laid it in the flags by the river's brink.

Moses' mother received a blue print from heaven that no other person before her had ever received: the revelation of the basket. Just as in the time of great need God gave the plan for the Ark to Noah, so the Lord also gave the revelation of the basket to the mother of baby Moses. Let's be honest, who before her had ever thought about putting a baby in a basket that was covered with pitch and then placing that basket in the River Nile with her only son – the very river that the king had said Hebrew babies would be thrown into and die!

What a woman of grace and courage she was. In those twelve weeks that followed the birth of her son she had sought God and prayed with every ounce of her being. As a result the plan of the basket was birthed form Heaven to earth. The basket was only to be for a short time but she never knew that when she was preparing it. She did not know that God had other destiny helpers ahead, she was simply obeying God with the revelation that she had received and was available to her in that moment. She did not have the big picture, only a tiny fragment of it and a desperate hope in a living God who can cause us to be victorious in every situation.

The "basket" is God's provision to every seeking soul in a time of great need. It is the unique answer God will provide to empower us to victory and to be overcomers in all situations, regardless of what the enemy is trying to do. God will cause us to rise gloriously above our circumstances, but it will require deep trust in Him and in His ways as we learn to walk on the waters of faith.

What must it have felt like for Moses' mum to place her beloved son in that basket? Please don't miss the sacrificial act of love and faith. In that moment she created an "altar" between Heaven and earth. An altar is a place of divine exchange. As she prayed and acted on her faith, relying totally in God, in that moment I believe Heaven paused and was silent and looked down in wonder at a woman trusting God above the reputation and the power and influence of the cruel and corrupt king pharaoh.

She trusted God in totality as she placed that baby in the basket and then lowered the basket into the Nile. It was a statement of life and trust in God and God would immediately reward this dear woman and intervene for her entire family. She was Moses' greatest destiny helper by giving him back to God. She came to the end of herself, of her own ability to change the situation but in doing so, she stepped into the fullness of Gods redemptive plan for her family.

Perhaps you are facing a situation with your child today and like Moses' mum you need to step back and give this entire circumstance and your child (no matter whether they are young or old) back into the loving arms of God. He has heard your prayers and He will answer. He is faithful in every scenario to those who love and trust Him.

The Sister (Miriam)

4And his sister stood afar off, to wit what would be done to him.

We cannot be sure what age Moses' sister was at the time of birth, only that she was his only sister since no other siblings are mentioned. We hear of Miriam, the sister of Moses, in later exploits of the family. We can assume this then is the same young woman. She is not a tiny child because she has the capacity to act and to speak as we will soon see. For now she is introduced to us in somewhat of an anonymous fashion and she is our third destiny helper.

Before we dig a little deeper into the story, we should consider what could be running through the mind of this young lady? She had loved her baby brother from the moment he was born. She had watched her mother nurse him for three months and she had prayed and held him tightly to herself, also reaching out to God in her tears.

As we meet her she was standing on the banks of the river Nile, watching her mum place her only brother in a tiny basket covered in pitch, and the baby drifted away down-stream. What must have gone through her mind? Did she wonder if her mother had lost her mind? Did tears run down her cheeks as thoughts of never seeing the baby again bombarded her? Did faith rise up in her? We can never know for sure this side of eternity, but we can put ourselves in her place and imagine the emotional turmoil. We must accede to her courage because she was not hidden from view as she stood on the river bank. She, too, was waiting for divine intervention in the life of her tiny brother.

The Daughter of Pharaoh

⁵ And the daughter of Pharaoh came down to wash herself at the river; and her maidens walked along by the river's side; and when she saw the ark among the flags, she sent her maid to fetch it.⁶ And when she had opened it, she saw the child: and, behold, the babe wept. And she had compassion on him, and said, This is one of the Hebrews' children.

Finally, we are about to meet the fourth and fifth category of destiny helpers in the early life of Moses namely the daughter of Pharaoh and the maidens who accompanied her.

The princess had gone down to the water to bathe and her handmaidens were with her. The daughter of Pharaoh is a woman in a position of power and influence. She was in a totally different realm to those we have met previously in our story. She did not work for a living as the midwives did neither was she yet a mother of any child. She was the privileged daughter of a cruel king, who must have been fully aware of the edict her father has passed concerning Hebrew baby boys. Now she found herself thrust into the centre of the drama without any kind of forewarning. She was from a different culture, she was not a Jew and yet she became a deliverer of a Hebrew baby boy who was just twelve weeks old.

She looked at the baby and noted from his circumcision that he was, indeed, a Hebrew. Her heart was moved by the compassion of God and she too, like the midwives, the mother and the sister before her now dug deep into the heart of God. We can only imagine what must have run through her mind as she thought about her father's words and now she was about to contradict him. Imagine, the king's daughter was about to countermand his instruction in full view of her maids!

The Maids

The princess spotted the small basket in the bull rushes and instructed her maids to go and fetch it from the water. The maids, by comparison to the daughter of Pharaoh, are most probably women of a low social status. We might consider them to have little or no influence or any power to change anything at all, yet in the plans of God they are used so strategically. They do not say anything. Their only job is to lift the baby in the basket. They are bridge builders on the journey of redemption. They do not need to say anything; they simply need to be in the right place at the right time. Their one action was instrumental in placing Moses in the presence of their mistress.

God reveals to us that He can use anyone at any time in any place to make a difference in the life of another. Even if our beginnings are humble, even if we are in a lowly place we are still capable of being used by Almighty God to change a life for His glory. The maids did not have oratory prowess or power, but they had the ability to lift up another. It was all God needed them to do and it made a difference to the baby Moses.

As we ponder Moses' beginnings I am reminded of a young lady I met from the Hindu caste system recently. She came to me requesting prayer. She mentioned that she was born-again, Spirit-filled and believed God had a great plan for her life. As we talked I discerned that she had been born into a low caste and upon enquiry she confirmed this. Despite her knowing by the word of God that she was not "less than", her cultural identity was attempting to usurp her Kingdom identity in this regard. She was struggling to get free of low self-worth. We prayed and God gloriously broke in. Her mind was healed. In that moment I was simply a maid, lifting up the life of another before the Lord, so that He might work out their redemption and freedom.

Returning to our story we now see an unexpected interaction unfolding between the daughter of Pharaoh and the sister of Moses. *7Then said his sister to Pharaoh's daughter, Shall I go and call to thee a nurse of the Hebrew women, that she may nurse the child for thee? 8 And Pharaoh's daughter said to her, Go. And the maid went and called the child's mother.9 And Pharaoh's daughter said unto her, Take this child away, and nurse it for me, and I will give thee thy wages. And the women took the child, and nursed it.*

Moses' sister found her voice and what a voice it turned out to be! The young lady who had stood silently by the river bank had been tactically positioned by God to see the baby lifted from the Nile and be placed before the princess. She wasted no time in drawing within ear shot of the princess. On hearing her comments about the baby being Hebrew, she asked Pharaoh's daughter if she would like her to go and find a wet nurse for the child. Just like the midwives before her, this young woman was fast acting and rushed to her brother's assistance. She knew how to ask the right question. Knowing how and when to ask the right question with the right heart motivation will always move the heart of God. Jesus often asked questions and answered other people's questions with a question, in order to reveal the wisdom of God in a situation or to reveal the motivation of a person's heart.

Straight away Pharaoh's daughter instructed Moses' sister to go and find a nurse. Of course, unknown to her, the young woman called upon her mother. Running breathless to the family home, perhaps finding her mother in silent tears wondering at the fate of her little boy she had just placed in the Nile but a few moments or hours before. What glory must have filled the home as the daughter told her mum to come quickly, tugging on her mother's arm, gasping to tell her what has just happened. Without hesitation the mother went with her daughter. They are a picture of the generations working together in the purposes of God. The two women ran to river bank there to be greeted by the king's daughter. She instructed Moses' mum to take the child away and nurse it on her behalf, even offering to pay the wet nurse for nurturing the baby! It is a joy when generations work together in Kingdom purposes. Like Jochebed and her daughter Miriam, God still has a great longing to see women of all ages and generations co-labour in the Kingdom.

It is the most astonishing intervention by God in the life of the baby Moses. The child was safely returned to his mother, his father, his sister and his home. Additionally, the family were financially blessed by the daughter of the king who issued the death edict in the first place! God's gracious miracle answer had come with such power and compassion to the family albeit it would be only for a time until Moses was to return to the court of Pharaoh.

Verse 10 tells us, *And the child grew, and she brought him unto Pharaoh's daughter, and he became her son. And she called his name Moses: and she said, Because I drew him out of the water.*

Here again the sacrificial love and trust of Moses' mother is evident for all to see. It was necessary for Moses to spend some time in the courts of Pharaoh, as part of the preparation for his destiny as the deliverer of the Hebrew people. His name 'Moses,' means 'drawn out'. God had used five groups of *women* as destiny helpers to ensure the nation was delivered into His glorious plans.

Take a moment to reflect on your own life and walk with God. Thank Him for all those who have come along at just the right time to do what God has mandated them to do or to say. Open your heart and mind also to the possibility of becoming a destiny helper to others.

Truly, as women, God can use us in in a myriad of ways in all of life's eventualities! We were created to be Destiny Helpers!

CHAPTER 2 - THE PRAYING MOTHER

ELISHA AND THE WIDOW

⁴Now there cried a certain woman of the wives of the sons of the prophets unto Elisha, saying, Thy servant my husband is dead; and thou knowest that thy servant did fear the LORD: and the creditor is come to take unto him my two sons to be bondmen.
² And Elisha said unto her, What shall I do for thee? tell me, what hast thou in the house? And she said, Thine handmaid hath not any thing in the house, save a pot of oil.
2 Kings 4

A mother's love is a powerful love. There are few forces on earth greater than the true love of a mum for her children. There is something I refer to as, "Mama Bear Syndrome," which is a tongue-in-cheek reference to the defensive reaction of a mother against anything threatening her children. It is seen in the world of animals in nature, and is also witnessed in human beings.

The woman of God we are meeting in this story is a woman of enormous "mama bear" proportions. She does not at first seem to be such a valiant warrior but as we consider the drastic nature of her circumstances and her incredible faith-filled responses we will not fail to be challenged, shaped and inspired to live more fully surrendered to God. Our faith will rise to another level.

Each one of us may face difficulties from time to time as we journey in life, but we can count on God to always offer us a means for deliverance and salvation. We, like the woman we are about to meet, simply need to learn how to be participators in our own miracle. We do the small that we can do and God does what only He can do.

What Do We Know About This Woman?

The writer of Second Kings opens the narrative by stating she was a *"certain woman of the sons of the prophets unto Elisha."* Since Elisha did not have any physical sons that we are aware of, the description must therefore refer to a spiritual relationship that existed between the woman's husband and Elisha. He was a spiritual son of Elisha the great prophet in Israel at that time. Her late husband was described as being God-fearing. In summary we know he was a servant of God, a prophet and a spiritual son of Elisha who was active in ministry prior to his death.

The woman's husband had died an unexpected and untimely death and she was in dire straits. She came to Elisha seeking urgent assistance. Not only had she suffered the loss of her husband, she was about to also face the loss of her two precious sons. She stated to Elisha that there were men on the way to take her two sons from her in payment for the debt that her husband had left behind. The young men would be required to work off the debt their father owed. If they were not able to do so, they would be relegated to a life of slavery and become slaves of the person to whom the debt was owed. Unfortunately, this was normal practise in their day.

We might ask ourselves how did a God-fearing servant of the Most High end up dying with such an amount of debt that his sons were about to be sold off? Did God abandon this family? Was there something the man of God had done wrong that had put his family in jeopardy? Wondrously, all our questions will be answered in the unfolding of this family's courageous story and we will discover the answers to be quite the reverse.

It would appear she had no one else to turn to and in her time of great need she sought the counsel of a spiritual parent that both she and her husband trusted. She is an example of wisdom to us: when all around is falling down don't seek the counsel of just anybody but instead turn to the voice of a trusted father or mother in the faith. Elisha knew the family. He was invested in them. His responses indicate he cared about them and he would have their best interests at heart. Unfortunately, not everyone is as scrupulous as Elisha was.

What Shall I Do For Thee?

2 And Elisha said unto her, What shall I do for thee? tell me, what hast thou in the house?

Elisha was obviously extremely concerned and deeply moved about the family's situation. His initial response was to ask the widow two questions. The first, *"What shall I do for thee?"* focuses on what Elisha thought he could personally and potentially do to help the woman and her sons. Perhaps he was looking at his wallet or money bag and wondering if he had the means himself to pay the debt. Perhaps he looked and found nothing or little. His motive was unquestionably admirable. His care, counsel and wisdom in asking the right questions were crucial. His faith to come alongside the family in a time of trauma was absolutely vital but nonetheless we will discover the answer did not lie in the wallet of Elisha.

What Can You Do For Yourself?

Elisha's second question to the woman, *"What has thou in the house?"* is a total turnaround from his initial position. His first question was centred round what he might have been able to do but it is as though he had an epiphany when he asked the woman the second question. Now the emphasis was not on what any other person could provide; now he asked her what she had in her hands that could be part of her own solution. This is an extremely different approach from the first question. We must shift our minds to another paradigm in order to see the enormity of what just happened. We are not in poverty even when we have great need. Women of God, we serve the God of the miraculous and He can provide in any and every situation.

The woman must have looked at the prophet with incredulity. Her husband was dead. Her sons were about to be taken from her. The man of God knew fully well she had nothing or she would have paid the debt already to prevent her family being removed from her. Why on earth would he ask her when he knew full well she had nothing? Or does she?

In times of trauma we can be overcome by emotion and overwhelmed by the consequences of others people's actions, such as a debt left that we must now take care of. In such times one's ability to think with a clear head can become fuddled. Not only that, the woman had suffered the major loss of her husband. She was attempting to deal with her own grief whilst the threat of those coming to seek usury was knocking at her door.

And she said, Thine handmaid hath not anything in the house, save a pot of oil.

In the sentence above there is a comma, and the comma was much more than a simple punctuation mark. The comma was the difference between life and death for this family. What precedes the comma was true: she didn't have anything of any earthly value in her house, but what followed the comma is more powerful and became a spiritual truth that unlocked the destiny and blessing of redemption for this sweet woman and her sons.

After the comma came five words, "*save a pot of oil.*" She had a pot of oil. It was a small pot of oil, it was not adequate in earthly terms to the task but it is all that she had. She had forgotten she even had that pot of oil until the prophet asked her the question. We can forget to remember that even in the most difficult of times, God has given each one of us something that become a key of resource to unlock blessing. The thing we dismiss as irrelevant, as nothing, as unimportant can become the catalyst for opening Heaven on our behalf. What do we have in our hands? What has God given to us? What equity do we possess? I do not refer here necessarily to finances although they are part of the dialogue, but also to spiritual keys of wisdom, to faith, to practical gifts and experience and to anointing. We all have something that in God's hands can unlock phenomenal blessing.

The Words of Instruction

3Then he said, Go, borrow thee vessels abroad of all thy neighbours, even empty vessels; borrow not a few. 4 And when thou art come in, thou shalt shut the door upon thee and upon thy sons, and shalt pour out into all those vessels, and thou shalt set aside that which is full.

Elisha, one of the greatest prophets to ever live did not give the woman a prophetic word or a piece of revelation. Interestingly, he gave her three words of instructions. These instructions were of paramount importance. He directed the woman of God to go and borrow as many receptacles as possible from her neighbours. He was quite insistent that she borrow many. His second instruction was that when she had obtained the vessels she must then take her sons, the little pot of oil and the borrowed vessels and go into a room, shut the door and pour out the oil into the bottles, the pots and pans till they were full up. The third instruction will come later in the story.

Let's pause for a moment. Elisha had just told the woman to go and knock on the doors of her neighbours and ask them for pots and pans. The woman was grieving! The debt collectors were on the way to take her sons. What kind of man or woman of God would seem so heartless or so stupid as to send a woman with nothing out to borrow pots and pans? That my friends, is the voice of unbelief and we may wonder afresh that this woman did not veer into unbelief but remarkably she found the grit and grace to go and do exactly what the spiritual father had suggested. In so doing she affirmed the importance of the relationship of trust between Elisha and the family.

No doubt her eyes were swollen from crying and grief; nonetheless she put her emotions to one side and focused on the task in hand. She had an instruction and she obeyed.

The instruction from Elisha would have amounted to little except that the woman of God trusted him and did as he bid. Can you imagine the faces of the neighbours? Who amongst us could deny that in any small community when a neighbour has passed away, we are all deeply aware of the loss of a family? Those doors she knocked on brought neighbours running who knew of the death of her husband. They might have thought her quite mad when she asked them, "Please can you lend me your pot?" Despite this they responded to her request for we know she did not come away empty handed. She was given many vessels and pots. She only borrowed them. Gloriously, there will be a time to take them back and things will have changed dramatically and for the better by then. For now we marvel at her capacity to hear and act upon Godly instruction.

What Will God Do With You?

5 So she went from him, and shut the door upon her and upon her sons, who brought the vessels to her; and she poured out. 6 And it came to pass, when the vessels were full, that she said unto her son, Bring me yet a vessel. And he said unto her, There is not a vessel more. And the oil stayed

Having gathered up the vessels, the woman obeyed the second instruction which was to taker her two sons and the oil and the pots and to go into a room and close the door, there to pour out the oil.

She could have told the man of God he was mad. She didn't have a blue print for what was about to happen but the realm of the miraculous was about to open to the woman and her sons in an unprecedented fashion. God was about to meet them in their corporate faith.

Consider these two dear sons. They had just lost their father, they knew that time was limited and that men were on the way to take them into captivity. They could have reviled their mother and ridiculed her. They could have been bitter that their father had left debt that was about to take their freedom but their hearts and minds were truly revealed as a family who loved and served God. They could have even tried to run away! But they were God-fearing and each one of them took their place and the boys quietly followed their mama into the little room where no one could see but the eyes of their Heavenly Father were watching every detail.

The door closed behind them. I'm certain Elisha prayed silently and with as much faith as he could muster somewhere nearby but for now it was time for the God of Elisha to reveal that He needed no man to take care of any debt. The woman took the oil and lifted the first container. Imagine the Father of Lights watching over this family and as that precious woman took the only thing of any financial value, the only thing she possessed as an asset and poured it out in faith, the love and power of our Heavenly Father exploded in that small room. The woman and her sons joined their faith together and as bottle after bottle was filled, the atmosphere of glory saturated their living space. They became participators in their own miracle. Overflow was happening and it seemed unstoppable. The only reason the oil stopped flowing was because they ran out of containers!

The Third Word of Instruction

7Then she came and told the man of God. And he said, Go, sell the oil, and pay thy debt, and live thou and thy children of the rest.

The story did not end with the miracle outpouring. There had to be proper administration and stewardship of the miracle. The debt collectors were still on the way to take the sons and so the woman went back to Elisha and he gave her the third and final instruction which was to go and sell all of the oil and then use the proceeds to pay her debt.

Legacy

There are several commas in the final sentence of the story that unlocked the fullness of honour with which God treated both the memory of the departed father and the legacy of the family were yet to live on. Elisha told the woman to sell the oil, and pay her debt, *and* live on the remainder. There was such an abundance in the miracle outpouring that there would be enough left for the entire family to live on for the foreseeable future.

The man had died in service to the Lord and God honoured his memory by ensuring his widow and sons were able to pay off the debt he had incurred and have enough for life and legacy.

Integrity

I love that the woman paid her debt. She did not run away from the debt. She did not pretend it did not exist; neither did she try to bury the debt when she became a woman of means. She did the right thing in stewardship of the miracle money God placed in her hands. She continues to be an example to us even in the manner in which she paid the outstanding bills and could then live rightly on the remainder.

I also admire the integrity of Elisha. He did not extort any kind of payment from the woman for assisting her. Some unscrupulous leaders today extort vast amounts of money from needy servants of God. It is predatory and a disgraceful way for so-called Christian leaders to conduct themselves.

I am sorry to say there are many abuses of the prophetic grace in churches throughout the world today and it is totally unacceptable. Wherever I encounter such abuses I expose them and give counsel and comfort to the abused and correction where necessary to the abuser. I have heard of instances when a prophet will give a person with a pressing condition or circumstance part of a "word". The prophetic morsel is designed to entice the person to then later attend an arranged prophetic meeting, where the "prophet" will then give the remainder of the prophecy for a sizeable fee. No payment, no prophecy. Atrocious! Thankfully there are many genuine and wonderful prophets who release blessing to

God's people in the global church and importantly should not be tarred with the brush of abuse.

I remind us the woman gave everything to God in a moment of tremendous faith despite her physical, financial, emotional and spiritual needs. She trusted God more than she feared her enemies. She observed and responded to the counsel of her husband's spiritual father. She was an example of resplendent faith and courage to her sons. What a blessing this family has become to the world of believers today. The testimony of this family did not only bless them but their entire community was positively influenced by what God had done in for them.

Their Family Testimony Revived a Community

We know that the woman of God had borrowed many containers from multiple households in her community in her family's time of deepest need. Now she was able to return those pots and pans to the neighbours who had contributed to the miracle by their simple provision of sharing what they, too, had in their hands. What seemed small and insignificant became a container for blessing.

Imagine now the faces of the neighbours as the woman and her sons returned the pitchers, the bowls etc. sharing with the neighbours of all that God had done. They had come with great need and now they returned with great blessing. This family's testimony, albeit birthed in the fire of pain and affliction, shone with the glory of God. They were not passive in the time of outpouring but actively engaged in their miracle with God.

God Can Never Run Out

God can never run out of provision for us. His provision became protection for the family. It also honoured the memory of the Godly father who had died in debt. We must remember that the reign of Jezebel had caused chaos and murder of the prophetic community. Perhaps this man had spent himself in protecting prophets in hiding? We will never know whether this was the case, but we can surmise as to how he most probably gave himself in totality in serving God. God could not allow His servant to die without honouring his family and leaving them with a spiritual and a physical legacy.

Let the nameless woman and her sons of 2 Kings mentor us in their example. May we, like them, lift up our eyes to the God of Heaven and earth when everything is crashing round about us and know His peace and provision.

[3]Thou wilt keep him in perfect peace, whose mind is stayed on thee: because he trusteth in thee. [4] Trust ye in the LORD for ever: for in the LORD JEHOVAH is everlasting strength: Isaiah 26

CHAPTER 3 - THE WORSHIPPING WOMAN

THE PROSTITUTE AT THE HOME OF SIMON THE PHARISEE

36 And one of the Pharisees desired him that he would eat with him. And he went into the Pharisee's house, and sat down to meat.
37 And, behold, a woman in the city, which was a sinner, when she knew that Jesus sat at meat in the Pharisee's house, brought an alabaster box of ointment,
Luke 7

The Woman

We are initially told very little about the woman who wept at the feet of Jesus, yet we can comprehend so much from the small amount of information that is made available to us. Verse 37 informs us that the subject of our story is female, that she is a sinner and that when she heard that Jesus was in the Pharisee's house, she came with a gift to meet Him. It all sounds predictable and the details somewhat banal – she could be any person, in any place really but this is not the moral of this profound encounter with Christ. We will discover the depths, the courage, the passion and the inspiration of this unlikely heroine of the faith. Truly, we may not know her name this side of Heaven, but that does not mean her response to the presence of Christ cannot teach us many things and inspire us.

The sinful woman's story speaks volumes to us of the compassion of Christ, the vastness of His grace and the interaction of the divine with humanity, no matter how depraved or hopeless the circumstance may be. She emerges from the most unlikely scenario to become an example of a worshipper whose extravagance and humility touched the heart of Jesus and caused her to find acceptance and salvation. She uttered not a word in the entire telling of the story, but her actions spoke louder than any words could have and they most certainly drown out the religious accusatory tones of the Pharisee and those others gathered at his home on the night that Christ came to dine there! She shows us there is hope for the hopeless in the heart of Almighty God. No one is beyond His saving grace.

A Woman of Reputation

We might consider her to be a woman of no reputation or, worse still, a woman of vile reputation. What is evident is that she is known to the people of the city. Her reputation, whatever that might have been, has most certainly preceded her to the home of the religious leader Simon the Pharisee. She could never have won any kind of popularity contest that is for sure! St Luke stated she was a "sinner," and it is thought by many Biblical scholars that this woman was actually a prostitute. The sex worker was coming to supper with the Lord Jesus and Jesus had no problem with that at all.

I don't believe for a second that people enter into prostitution because they have nothing better to do, or because they enjoy sex. I recall the first time I visited Corton Vale Women's prison in Scotland as a part time prison chaplain many years ago. I was so surprised by how young the women inmates were, and taken aback by the number who had babies with them in prison. I was informed that a large proportion of the women who were in prison were there because they had substance abuse issues and got involved in prostitution to pay for drugs or alcohol addictions. Others had found themselves financially destitute and in desperation had turned to the sex industry to try to make ends meet. Whilst yet others were victims of modern day trafficking.

All of this to say prostitution is not a desirous occupation. It takes a certain catalogue of disastrous circumstances for a person to end up in this positon. Our nameless woman gives us food for thought. She wasn't a prostitute for the enjoyment of it. She was likely alone or had others to support financially without the help of a husband. The opinions of other men and women would have disqualified her from meeting the Lord, but her genuine hunger to encounter God cancelled out every one of their objections. We mustn't let the opinion of other people stop us from meeting with the living God.

The Alabaster Box

It is erroneous for us to think of the woman at the home of Simon as being Mary the sister of Martha, whose brother Lazarus was raised back to life by Jesus just prior to His entering Jerusalem before His crucifixion. Mary of Bethany was only ever praised by Christ as being a devout believer, whereas the narrative of Luke chapter seven leaves us in no doubt of the lack of piety in the sinful woman prior to her meeting Christ. The sinful woman at the supper table could not bring herself to look at Christ, remaining behind Him until He turned to her later in our story. By contrast Mary came boldly before the feet of Christ to anoint Him with the spices and oils that had been saved for the time of His burial. The timing of the supper at the Pharisee's home was different to the timing of Mary breaking open her alabaster box. Christ acknowledged that Mary's gift was worth at least one year's wages, whilst the ointment contained in the alabaster box of the unknown woman was most likely worth very little given her lack of means. When Mary poured out her perfume her action is criticised and reviled by Judas, whilst the story of the sinful woman made no mention of Judas being present at all. We can conclude logically that this is not the same woman. (See John 11 for Mary's anointing of Christ)

The Gift of 'Cheap' Perfume

I would like us to ponder what it took for the nameless woman to come to the home of the religious leader. It was not an accident, but a deliberate and intentional act on her part. She had heard Jesus was coming to Simon's house and she made her way there, ensuring that she did not come empty handed.

It sounds a thing of no consequence to say she heard Jesus was in town and she decided to see what all the fuss was about, but we must delve deeper into her psyche and explore her life.

Let's consider those who would be at Simon's home – Simon himself is a respected religious leader, and no doubt most of the people attending the supper would be men and women of influence and power. Now think about the probability that this woman was a prostitute, a "low life" in the minds of those who were the guests. It was a costly decision for her to go. She might not have any kind of integrity of reputation, but I'm sure even she didn't want to lose the precious little dignity she had. Attending the home of a religious leader potentially opened her up for insult, slander and more rejection than she was already accustomed to in life. Still she chose to go and see who was this Jesus of whom she had evidently heard something significant? Whatever she knew of Christ, it could not have been much but it was enough to ignite a spark of hope in her. She is an example of faith that we might not be influenced by the opinions of others. When we take just one step of faith towards Christ, we cannot fail to be lifted up in His love as we will see.

To her great credit she did not go empty handed to visit the Master. She took with her an alabaster box of ointment. It takes no great stretch of the imagination to surmise that it was not expensive nard that lay within, for she had not the means to purchase it. It is much more likely to have been cheap perfume. Given that she was a sex worker, it is likely that she used perfume to try and help her attract clients. So we have the possibility that the alabaster box of perfume is actually what she would have adorned herself with to go to "work" and this is the same scent she is now brought with her to the Lord. Whilst this is conjecture, it is not beyond the realms of possibility. It might not have been an expensive scent but it was a costly decision to take it to the home of the Pharisee. Armed with her box and her perfume she wove her way through the dark and bustling city streets to bring herself to the appointed place and enters into Simon's home. God will always see to the heart of a matter.

Come Dine with Me

We might well ask how could a woman of such ill repute (or any other stranger for that matter) enter into the home of a respected religious leader and encounter an honoured guest when they had not been invited to the supper. In the culture of the day it was normal practise that influential leaders would invite guests of honour to their home for supper. It was also accepted practise that a small number of uninvited guests from the community were permitted to be in attendance, sitting some way of from the main gathering. They were not allowed to speak, but a few could be present to witness the supper banquet and listen in to the conversation of these most esteemed persons. This is the reason why it would appear that the woman was able to gain access so easily. As we read on we will discover there was much more to her ability to approach the Person of the Lord than we first realise.

She Fell At His Feet

38 And stood at his feet behind him weeping, and began to wash his feet with tears, and did wipe them with the hairs of her head, and kissed his feet, and anointed them with the ointment.

We must not be tempted to rush through the wording or we will miss the significance of many important details. She had entered into a difficult and stressful environment, where it was likely that most everyone except the Lord knew who she was by dint of her reputation. She was aware of what they thought of her. As she arrived people were either ignoring her or gaping open-mouthed at her tenacity. She had the gift of the alabaster box with perfume in her hands and she was temporarily at a loss as to what to do next.

All of this changed in the blink of an eye as she beheld the Lord Jesus Christ. Something in His gracious acceptance of her caused her once tough exterior to break down. She was utterly overwhelmed by His love. Perhaps for the first time in her life she had found acceptance without having to pay any price. A Love without compromise had caught her unaware and she could find no proper response other than to fall at His feet. She dared not stand before Him. She was swallowed up simultaneously in waves of forgiveness and love and at the same time she was radically aware of His holiness and the conviction in her heart. She fell at His feet and stayed there for what seemed like an endless age until He called her to stand.

If she had managed to go unnoticed up till now, then there is little doubt that from here on in she was the centre of attention whether she desired to be or not. She was not attention-seeking but she was transfixed by His presence and could not lift her gaze from His feet as all stared at her in total unbelief.

She wept without end and washed His dusty feet with her tears. Imagine all her working life she had endeavoured never to allow anyone close enough to see her pain. She would normally have done anything not to let "them" (the haters) see her cry but now before the Master she let go of the avalanche of tears that she had supressed till now.

Perhaps you, precious reader, have some tears you need to let go of too? I met a women in Poland a couple of years ago whose face was hardened with hatred until she let Jesus in. When we met she shared with me how she hated her son. I told her, "No, you don't hate him, you are just in pain." Eventually this precious woman chose to forgive herself and her son and tears cascaded down her face washing away years of disappointment and hurt. She was unrecognisable by the end of the prayer. Her countenance was literally shining with the love of God. Beautiful reader, if you have pain let it go now and give it to the Lord. He is waiting to wipe away every tear and to redeem those lost years.

The woman wiped away the grime from Christ's feet with her hair and kissed His feet anointing them with the perfume that she had brought with her. Her actions could easily have been perceived as sexually promiscuous, but the intent and the purity of her heart were laid bare before the King and He did not reject her.

Simon the Pharisee

39Now when the Pharisee which had bidden him saw it, he spake within himself, saying, This man, if he were a prophet, would have known who and what manner of woman this is that toucheth him: for she is a sinner.

Simon understood full well that the actions of the woman were not the most appropriate, and in his opinion they were certainly not suitable to be received without rebuke by a religious leader such as the Lord Jesus Christ. Scripture clearly stated that the Pharisee is *thinking* out loud, but he was not *speaking* out loud nonetheless his thoughts betrayed him. It would appear that Simon did not have noble intent when he invited the Lord for supper. He was simply checking Jesus out with a somewhat cynical and careless attitude. Simon was concerned about potential contamination but Christ is only ever concerned about our transformation in His presence and by the power of His love.

And Jesus Answering Said …

40And Jesus answering said unto him, Simon, I have somewhat to say unto thee. And he saith, Master, say on. 41 There was a certain creditor which had two debtors: the one owed five hundred pence, and the other fifty. 42 And when they had nothing to pay, he frankly forgave them both. Tell me therefore, which of them will love him most? 43 Simon answered and said, I suppose that he, to whom he forgave most. And he said unto him, Thou hast rightly judged.

It both delights and astounds me that Jesus answered Simon as though Simon had spoken out loud whilst in actuality Simon had simply been *thinking* "out loud." Jesus had discerned his heart attitude and questionable motivation. Nonetheless, the Lord was wise and kind even in how he dealt with Simon. Lest we forget, there was a group of guests hanging on every word of what is about to be said, the woman was still weeping behind the feet of Jesus and Simon was in front of Him. Every eye was on these three.

The Lord engaged Simon in an allegorical conversation from which Jesus taught and demonstrated mercy. He asked Simon hypothetically if two men owed a certain man money and both had their debts cancelled, which of the two would be most grateful. Logically, Simon answered the one with the greater debt. Jesus affirmed this was the correct answer.

Do You See This Woman?

⁴⁴And he turned to the woman, and said unto Simon, Seest thou this woman?

Jesus asked Simon if he could see the woman. It seems a silly question because of course he could see the woman, everyone could see the woman! So the question asked by Christ is not about whether or not she was visible to Simon. The question goes much deeper. It is about asking Simon if he could see the woman in the way that Jesus could. Simon, can you see beyond her reputation and her apparently unsuitable actions to her heart? Simon can you lay aside your prejudice and bias and your fear of being contaminated by her sin and see the purity of her heart? Can you see the humility behind her actions? Simon what do you see? Can you see her as I see her? It behoves us to do likewise. Do we see people as God sees them? Do we even see ourselves as God sees us?

Can you imagine? The Lord of Glory now turned to the woman. You will recall she was positioned behind Him and had fallen at His feet (verse 38). In order to speak with her face-to-face Jesus naturally had to turn round and in doing so He now placed His back to Simon. The woman had the full attention of Christ. He still did not speak directly to her, but instead addressed Simon further.

I entered into thine house, thou gavest me no water for my feet: but she hath washed my feet with tears, and wiped them with the hairs of her head. 45 Thou gavest me no kiss: but this woman since the time I came in hath not ceased to kiss my feet. 46 My head with oil thou didst not anoint: but this woman hath anointed my feet with ointment.

Despite the fact that we have established spectator guests were permitted at such gatherings, we must pause to understand why Jesus took time to discuss the woman's actions. He firstly mentioned that Simon had given no water for His feet, but that the lady had wept, wiped his feet with her hair and anointed them with her perfume. It is prudent to note that the custom of the day would be to wash the feet of an honoured guest. In the heat of the Middle East, with dust, animal droppings etc. it was only right to wash and refresh the guest's feet. This act of washing the feet was reserved for the lowliest of the household servants. Simon had failed to provide anyone to wash the Lord's feet, despite having spuriously invited Him as a guest of honour but the unknown woman had seen only honour in taking the lowest place before Christ to wash His feet.

Jesus had not been given the seat reserved for the guest of honour, which should have been at the top table. If you can, imagine a U-shape configuration at which the shorter part of the U-shape was the top table where the chief guest should have reclined. In Jesus' day people did not sit at the table, rather they reclined horizontally. This would be the part of the table which was furthest part away from the public and any entrance door way. The fact that the woman could reach to Jesus' feet at all, shows us that Simon had not given the seat of honour to Jesus otherwise the woman could not have come up behind Him, knelt down and washed them. Simon had utterly disrespected Jesus in the seating arrangements.

Jesus then pointed out to Simon (and all others within earshot) that Simon had not greeted Him with a kiss, but from the moment of His entry into the home, the sinful woman had not stopped kissing His feet. Once again the cultural mandate of the day was to meet and greet an esteemed guest with a kiss. Simon's lack of a kiss for the King is evidence of His total disregard for the King of glory. He had little or no love in his heart for Jesus.

The Lord then reminded Simon that he had not anointed His head with oil, yet the woman had poured out her perfumed ointment on His feet. This was another glaring hospitality omission on the part of Simon because every honoured guest was anointed with perfume on arrival at the home.

With each statement Christ hammered home the truth of Simon's glaring protocol of neglect and contrasted the unadulterated beauty of the sinful woman's worship at His feet. She, in her lowly position, had done more for Christ in Heaven's protocol than Simon or any of the other guests. Never underestimate your act of love to and for Christ. It is invaluable to the Lord of glory.

It was only now at this point that the Lord addressed the woman who has been at His feet the entire time. Jesus addressed the issue of salvation for her saying, *47 Wherefore I say unto thee, Her sins, which are many, are forgiven; for she loved much: but to whom little is forgiven, the same loveth little.*

Jesus left Simon and every other person in no doubt that this woman had loved Him beyond her means. Her honest, gutsy and misunderstood actions were not misplaced as she had worshipped Him when no other could or would. The Lord's final words were a double-edged sword. He affirmed she had loved much and therefore was forgiven, He cut through the political farce of Simon's invite and stated that those who love little have likewise been forgiven little. Jesus rebuked Simon's pretence in this way.

Salvation by Faith not by Works

Finally, Jesus spoke directly to the woman. *'Thy sins are forgiven.'*

What a moment of grace and mercy as the power of the Kingdom message of forgiveness and acceptance burst into the earth realm with those four simple words. The woman that we met at the beginning of supper is not the woman who takes her leave of us at the end.

She pushed through enormous adversity to meet with Christ and she was not disappointed. People had tried to get in her way, life had got in the way because her life had been hard but she desperately needed a change. She was so tired of the past and the present.

She didn't speak a word, but she didn't need to. There was a message of contrition and genuine repentance behind her tears. This woman came into the presence of a holy God of love and she responded with legitimate humility, reaching out with her faith that had no words but lacked no impact and Jesus accepted her. Her life was transformed, on earth and in the life to come.

We can confidently assert that her salvation was the result of her faith. It was not that she was rewarded because of the works of worship but because of faith. *50 And he said to the woman, Thy faith hath saved thee; go in peace.*

It was not her works but *her faith that had saved* her and Jesus released her with a word of peace. Those who grumbled at the supper table could not understand because they were as spiritually blind as Simon the Pharisee. They had questioned who was it that could forgive sins? God used the most unlikely woman to become a heroine of faith.

A woman, whose life could not have been further removed from the atmosphere of worship, became the centre of a worship-filled response to Jesus that changed her life forever. She entered the house hated and rejected. She left loved and accepted. She came in without hope but she left with hope overflowing. She came just as she was and it was enough for Christ.

She was transformed and just like her we can never remain the same when we encounter Jesus with genuine hearts full of love. Today take a moment to fall in love with your Saviour all over again.

If, for any reason, you are reading this and you don't yet know Christ as your personal Saviour and Lord pray this prayer with me now,

"Dear Lord Jesus, I come to you as a sinner and ask forgiveness for my sins. I believe you died for me on the Cross and I receive forgiveness for every sin I have ever committed and I release forgiveness to everyone who has ever sinned against me. I choose to turn from my old way of life and I joyfully step into my new life as your Disciple. Fill me to overflowing with your Holy Spirit, teach me how to pray and to read your word, use me in your Kingdom to share your love, grace and mercy with others. Thank you that from today my name is written in the Book of Life, that I am yours forever because of covenant through Christ. In Jesus' name. Amen

CHAPTER 4 - THE WOMAN BENT OVER FOR 18 YEARS

10 And he was teaching in one of the synagogues on the Sabbath.
11 And, behold, there was a woman which had a spirit of infirmity eighteen years, and was bowed together, and could in no wise lift up herself.
12 And when Jesus saw her, he called her to him, and said unto her, Woman, thou art loosed from thine infirmity.
13 And he laid his hands on her: and immediately she was made straight, and glorified God.
Luke 13

The Setting

10 And he was teaching in one of the synagogues on the Sabbath.

Jesus was teaching in an unnamed synagogue and it happened to be on the Sabbath. Our Master, Messiah, Rabbi, was teaching and preaching about the Kingdom of God from the word of God. We do not know on what topic He was sharing. We know not if it was the Torah, the Prophets, the Psalms, the historicity of the Jewish people, or the poetic verses but Jesus was teaching and the word of God was changing the atmosphere where everyone sat under His teaching. We must never underestimate the power of the word of God preached with apostolic anointing and authority.

It does not say it was a special healing service or that the power of God was present to heal the sick but we will discover that because of the presence of Jesus, the power of God was indeed present and He healed a dear woman who had been afflicted for eighteen years. Where Jesus is there can and always will be miracles! Let your faith rise up even now for your own miracle in Jesus' lovely name.

The Woman

11 And, behold, there was a woman which had a spirit of infirmity eighteen years, and was bowed together, and could in no wise lift up herself.

We are not acquainted with how the writer knew the woman had been ill for eighteen years. We do not know if Jesus received a word of knowledge about her situation or whether St Luke was simply recollecting the miracle of healing after the event and posthumously added pertinent details. However, we do know conclusively that the person Jesus was about to heal was a woman.

The Greek word *gune* is used throughout the New Testament and means 'woman' and can be specific for a 'wife'. We have no way of knowing if this lady was married, but our logical conclusion is perhaps not since no husband is mentioned in the Scripture. It may be she was once married but if so her husband had died and she was left a widow.

Keep Going to Church!

This was a woman who had been potentially ignored for eighteen years and had suffered a great deal during that time. She strikes me as a solitary figure, isolated, in pain and yet she is not painted as a self-pitying person. Far from being so, we find this dear woman in church! So many people stop going to church when something goes wrong in their lives but not this woman! No. She kept on coming to church, she kept on trusting God and we will shortly see how the Lord God rewarded her faith and her patience and her longsuffering. She is a model to us in virtue and in courage.

If you came to this chapter feeling in any way down or depressed or alone and in pain you can be assured that the same Jesus who healed this woman, will also rise up as your

Healer today. There is nothing beyond His saving grace. We just need to position ourselves in His presence in order to access His great power. We need to lay all thoughts of self-pity behind us and believe in the power of God to restore.

The woman needed a Deliverer and in truth, so do every one of us at some point in our lives whether we are male or female. She was evidently devout and pious, for we find her in church and her response to Christ is that of a believing woman. It is my conviction she had never been absent from the family of God in those eighteen years of suffering. Yet the family of God had been absent from her in her hour of need but now Jesus had come to the right the wrongs of many years of suffering.

This woman reminds me of a lovely lady I met in Uganda some years ago. Her name was Ann Margaret and for the first five days of the leadership conference we were ministering at she was always one of the first to respond. What was remarkable was that Ann Margaret could not walk. Instead she placed a pair of old worn leather sandals on her hands and on her hands and knees she would crawl to the front of the tent. My colleague and I saw her straight away but the Lord told us to wait to pray for her. On the final day Margaret came faithfully again to the altar, which was quite a feat given that there were around 1,000 people in that conference held outside under tents, who were also jostling as they approached the altar.

We held Ann Margaret and we prayed with every fibre of our being in faith she would be healed. Many times we have witnessed God do remarkable healing miracles but on this particular day Ann Margaret was not fully healed but she look at us and smiled and said, "If not today, then on another day my Jesus will heal me," and proceeded to crawl away on all fours with more internal dignity than most able-bodied persons could ever display.

My fellow minister and I wept at the example of faithfulness and faith she was to us in that moment. We bless God that

Ann Margaret taught us more about the goodness of God in her temporarily unhealed condition that we could ever have imagined.

Returning to our nameless woman in Scripture, we acknowledge she was sitting under the word of God when Jesus reached out and healed her. The Bible states that the woman had a "spirit of infirmity." Infirmity, Gk. *astheneia* means feebleness of body or mind, malady, weakness, infirmity, moral frailty, disease and/or sickness. This word leaves us in no doubt of the severity of her affliction.

It is described as a spirit, Gk. *pneuma* meaning in this case the malady had a spiritual source, and we understand that the source of suffering is Satan not God. Jesus affirmed this later in the dialogue when He stated she had been bound by Satan for eighteen years (see verse 18).The dear woman was bent over, unable to stand up. She could not help herself and it seemed no one else either wanted to or was able to until Jesus arrived on the scene.

The Healing

12 And when Jesus saw her, he called her to him, and said unto her, Woman, thou art loosed from thine infirmity.13 And he laid his hands on her: and immediately she was made straight, and glorified God.

It behoves us to tarry for a few moments in unpacking what happened next.   First of all, *"Jesus saw her."* Let the practicality of her condition now dictate logical thinking on our part. *How* was Jesus able to see her? She was bent over, doubled in two, she couldn't straighten up and she was amongst a crowd of people in the synagogue who neither cared nor contended for her to have an especially visible position. If they had cared, she would already be healed.

She was not gazing lovingly into Jesus' eyes, because she was physically unable to lift her head.   In her bent down condition, in the midst of many Jesus saw her. This is remarkable in itself. The heart of this woman, her faith to be in church to hear the word of God, her attitude and her virtue shouted to the King of Glory and He discerned her. It was not a seeing by dint of natural eyesight but recognition of the grace upon her life that brought her into the gaze of the living God.

Next the Bible states, "*He called her to Him.*" Once again, we wisely pause. Jesus could have simply spoken a word and she would have been healed right where she was bent over. We might ask ourselves, why did Jesus not go to her? I think He wanted to reposition her in a multitude of ways and it began by relocating her even within the physicality of the synagogue.

She Crossed the Gender Gap

We remind ourselves that men and women were not seated in the same areas within the building. For her to reach to Christ, she would first have had to cross over into the men's section. I reflect that even in the midst of this woman's healing, we can identify that Jesus is also doing something remarkable to heal women today, to lift them up from being downtrodden in any capacity and to restore them to healing and wholeness in every way including that of gender abuse issues.

This lady lived in a time where women in society were not even considered to be reliable witnesses. Now the Lord was calling her and what courage it must have taken for her to shuffle from where she was to where He needed her to be. Jesus was about to display His great power and love in and through her. He was in no way trying to embarrass her. We will momentarily see the truth is astonishing in its impact.

The woman was a Jew and it was the Sabbath and she was well aware of the conventions, rituals and rules of the day. She was flowing contra-wise to the religious culture by crossing over into the section where the men were seated in synagogue. Jesus used this woman's testimony to be a mould breaker. She had no idea what was about to happen next but she trusted the Lord and obeyed His call. She set her mind on going beyond where she was able to be.

The woman made her way painstakingly to Jesus. I expected you could have heard a pin drop in the synagogue and every eye was on the woman and on Jesus.

The Lord spoke to her and said, *Woman, thou art loosed from thine infirmity.*

He did not say her name, He did not yet call her daughter, but instead He simply told her she was loosed from the infirmity that had bound her up for almost two decades.

He spoke the word 'loosed;' Gk. *apoluo* is to be free fully, relieved, released, dismissed, pardoned, divorced, departed from, forgiven, let go, loosed, put or sent away, and to be set at liberty. Wow! That is quite a word that Jesus used in those seven words that were about to undo eighteen years of grief and pain. Women of God when Jesus says we are set free, we are free indeed!

Immediately

Jesus placed His hands upon the lady in prayer and she was immediately healed and she straightened up as power flowed from the Lord to her. If you ever have seen a person who has suffered for a long time from any kind of bone disease you will know that it is impossible for such a thing to happen without divine intervention and a creative healing miracle.

I have been blessed on many occasions to witness the miracle-working power of Jesus in meetings, in churches, in prisons, hospitals, back streets, business places and colleges and schools in nations all over the world. Missing bones growing and deformed bones being realigned, ear drums appearing where none previously existed, blind eyes opening, the lame walking to name but a few. Jesus is Healer! He can grow limbs; He can cause deformed bones to normalise and cancers to disappear.

She Praised God

When Jesus laid His hands on her, the dual effect of His words and His anointing upon her once-broken body brought the power of Heaven upon this precious woman and she was perfectly and suddenly healed. Her back straightened up, the bones were realigned and every swelling, each pain and all effects of the long suffering were taken away. It was such a glorious moment and her immediate response was to glorify and praise God as she straightened up. She finally had her miracle. God could not deny this precious soul. Jesus saw her! Jesus called her! Jesus healed her! But there was yet more He was doing.

When people are healed in such a manner they are rarely quiet. Perhaps she was, but my experience has been that when people are healed in this way they get so excited. They jump up and down because they cannot contain the joy of being set free. I'm thrilled that this is what I have witnessed, although I am simultaneously reminded of one occasion when upon hearing a bona fide resurrection testimony people fell into unbelief.

We will consider unbelief shortly because the initial response by the majority in the synagogue was not what we would hope for in the company of those who love and believe in God. However, I thank God that the flagship response was a joyous, humble, grateful heart that celebrated the God of miracles who had just healed her. Any other sound was drowned out in the majesty of her acknowledging the source of her healing.

The Synagogue Ruler

14 And the ruler of the synagogue answered with indignation, because that Jesus had healed on the Sabbath day, and said unto the people, There are six days in which men ought to *work: in them therefore come and be healed, and not on the Sabbath day. ¹⁵ The Lord then answered him, and said, Thou hypocrite, doth not each one of you on the Sabbath loose his ox or his ass from the stall, and lead him away to watering?*

The first person to speak after the woman was the synagogue ruler, whom we might describe as the religious spiritual leader of the house. What then did he say? How did he act? Apparently he reacted with indignation, Gk. *agnakteo* meaning he was sorely displeased! The word comes from the Greek for 'much' (*agan*) and 'grief' (*achtos*). He was deeply offended by what Jesus had done.

Ignoring the miracle healing and ignoring Jesus, he turned towards the congregation and addressed them. He insisted there were six days in which people could be healed but that the Sabbath day was for rest only. If we do the maths we can easily work out that over a period of eighteen years in which the woman had been so deeply afflicted and affected by suffering, there were a total of 6,570 days in which she could have been healed. If we deduct a potential 936 Sabbath days as days of "rest", it leave us with a possible 5,634 days on which the Rabbi or any member of his congregation could have prayed for her healing but they did not! More than five and a half thousand opportunities were missed to care for this woman amongst their own church family. What an admonition!

Sabbath in Israel

When I last visited Israel we were driving through the Jewish quarter in Jerusalem just before sun set. Our driver was eager to get through quickly because once the Sabbath commenced we would be unable to pass through the gates into the area where we were staying until after Sabbath ended 24 hours later. We witnessed Jewish fathers rushing to Synagogue with small boys in tow as Sabbath was about to commence.

Returning to the hotel I entered into the lift and was joined by two sweet Jewish women. It was not a 'special lift' to be used on Sabbath day, so they asked me if I could help and press the button for the floor they needed. The 'special lifts' for Sabbath stopped on every floor automatically without any buttons needing to be pressed but this hotel did not have them.

On Sabbath the Jewish people are not permitted to press the button to stop the lift because it would be seen as an act of work. This would be regarded as breaking the command to take rest on Sabbath day. They must therefore rely on the kindness of another to press the button on a lift so they may exit on the relevant floor. The alternative is that they use the special lifts that stop on every floor if and when they are available.

This is just a simple example of modern day adherence of the principle of not "working" on Sabbath. It was this type of mind set that the religious ruler was embroiled in. It gives us a glimpse in our story of the enormity of what the religious leader perceived as a breaking of the commandment on the Sabbath day by Christ.

Undeterred Jesus turned His attention from the woman to the synagogue ruler and in front of everyone called him a hypocrite. Gk. *hupokrites*: an actor under an assumed character (stage player) i.e. fig a "hypocrite."

We can summarise that in the Greek explanation of the word Jesus had just accused the Rabbi of being a fake and a sham, who was acting in front of people. He was a liar in how he represented God. He was a selfish man and no better than a thief because he was a robber of God's mercy to His people. Jesus called him out on the ridiculous nature of his objection, (the ruler having cited the Sabbath rest as a reason for the woman not to be prayed for and receive her miracle). Jesus stated that even he (the ruler) would not hesitate to take his cattle and donkey from their stall and lead them away to provide them with water when they were thirsty. How much more will God lead His people to rivers of living water in salvation and healing miracles? Jesus is Lord of the Sabbath, it is not the Sabbath that lords it over Christ.

A Daughter of Abraham

16 And ought not this woman, being a daughter of Abraham, whom Satan hath bound, lo, these eighteen years, be loosed from this bond on the Sabbath day?

One might think this would be the end of the dialogue but Jesus had something further to say and it will blow our minds!

Having previously addressed the lady as simply a 'woman,' the Lord went on to affirm her as a "daughter of Abraham" in front of the entire people. In so doing Jesus confirmed her Jewish identity, her legitimacy, her position as a daughter and an heir of God.

Jesus affirmed her identity, her lineage, her family and that she was not without a father. But the Lord was doing much more than encouraging the woman. He was breaking more bonds and barriers in the minds of the people present. We know this because they have a change of heart and a change of mind.

As a daughter of Abraham the woman was an inheritor of the 6-fold blessing God spoke to Abraham, which is:

1. I will make of thee a great nation
2. I will bless thee,
3. And make thy name great;
4. And thou shalt be a blessing:
5. And I will bless them that bless thee, and curse him that curseth thee:
6. And in thee shall all families of the earth be blessed.

This woman who had been invisible to everyone for at least eighteen years was now being raised up in the midst of a religious battle, as a legitimate daughter of God not only physical healed but with a spiritual capacity to bless others also. Her physical healing was just the beginning of many blessings. God had use for this dear woman.

Jesus had just railed at the ruler and told him he was like an imposter before the people of God. In stark contrast Christ affirmed the woman in her Kingdom identity and in her Kingdom destiny. She was not only a woman healed, but a woman who was an ambassador and an advocate for the Kingdom of God! Wow!

We read in Galatians 3 how, *13 Christ hath redeemed us from the curse of the law, being made a curse for us: for it is written, Cursed is every one that hangeth on a tree: 14 That the blessing of Abraham might come on the Gentiles through Jesus Christ; that we might receive the promise of the Spirit through faith.*
Because Christ has gone to the Cross and ascended to the right hand of the Father, the blessing for the Jewish woman is now also the blessing of the spiritual descendants of Abraham, which is the believing church, Gentile and Jew together in Christ.

The Crowd have a Change of Heart and a Change of Mind

17 And when he had said these things, all his adversaries were ashamed: and all the people rejoiced for all the glorious things that were done by him. Luke 13

When Jesus had finished speaking, the bible stated that ALL His former adversaries in the synagogue were ashamed and thereafter ALL the people rejoiced for ALL the wonderful and glorious works of God they had witnessed.

Adversary *Gk. antikeima* to be opposite, to be adverse (repugnant). It is not the same word for enemies, Gk. *echtos* from to hate, hateful, odious or act of hostility, foe, esp. the adversary Satan.

The people in the synagogue had been led by a false type of shepherd and they had lacked understanding up till now. They did not hate Jesus, but they initially rejected the healing and opposed Him because they did not know any better. However, when Jesus acted with compassion to heal the woman and when He spoke and corrected the ruler there eyes were opened to the reality of the mercy and love of God, which is available 24-7, 365 days a year. Once they gained this understanding, every one of them joined in rejoicing and celebrating the woman's miracle. They were no longer adversaries, but they were friends of God and they gladly received Messiah's ministry. We must model the love of Christ in order to see the love of Christ in others.

Mould Breaker, Bridge Builder, Female Advocate

The nameless woman of our story was a mould breaker and Jesus used her life to build a bridge from His heart to reach many others. Her miracle had been long in coming but God was faithful and true to her in the end. She never gave up on God and she never gave up on church. Crucially, God never gave up on her. She had a quiet faith and a courage that is our pattern to follow yet she was utterly bold in her responses to Christ even flying in the face of condemnation for breaking "religious protocol."

The woman became an advocate for women's rights without even realising it. We meet her bent over, beaten down and suffering but by the time our story ended she is standing straight, totally restored and her testimony was already bearing good fruit.

We can applaud her for many reasons. Even before she was healed, she crossed over from the women's section to the men's section in the synagogue and in so doing she unwittingly broke some mouldy minds-sets of gender inequality and religious pompousness. She crossed over and created a bridge of hope. She walked bent but she walked bold. She was broken but determined that nothing and no one would stop her walk of freedom towards her Saviour.

What a champion of faith!

I am certain there are many millions more women like her in the world today.

CHAPTER 5 - THE WIDOW AT NAIN

[13] And when the Lord saw her, he had compassion on her, and said unto her, Weep not.
Luke 11

The story of the raising of the widow's son at Nain by the Lord Jesus Christ is of exceptional comfort and value to every believer. It is of special encouragement and significance to those who are mourning and those who are caring for those who are grieving and also to those who are struggling with overwhelming emotional responses to trauma and pain.

As I revisited this portion of Scripture some time ago, I came to a phenomenal understanding that there were two miracles that day in Nain; two resurrections that were required and not just one. Please read on and be blessed and encouraged today.

Emotions Led By The Spirit of God

As women we need to be encouraged in the word of God, to be edified by it, to be strengthened by it, to be shaped, moulded and transformed by it rather than allowing our emotions to be the barometer by which we live. Emotions are a gift from God but they must operate under the leading of the Holy Spirit. May God help us today in the power of His word anointed by the Holy Spirit.

[11] And it came to pass the day after, that he went into a city called Nain; and many of his disciples went with him, and much people.

It was a busy time of ministry and most fruitful! This introductory Scripture reminds us that Jesus was coming from healing the Centurion's servant in another region. There had been a great healing as a result of the Centurion's faith and his comprehending of the delegated authority of Christ. Just the word from Christ meant the man who had been dying was now healed. A crowd went with Jesus, including those near to Him (His disciples) and also a wider group of people. This group of people encountered the widow of Nain and the group of mourners who are with her. They were coming in an atmosphere of corporate faith meeting a group of people who desperately needed those who can stand with them in such faith.

Utterly Alone

12 Now when he came nigh to the gate of the city, behold, there was a dead man carried out, the only son of his mother, and she was a widow: and much people of the city was with her.

This is the only child of the woman. Not only does she not have any other children, she is utterly alone. There are no siblings to mourn the loss of their brother, such as Martha and Mary when their brother Lazarus died and they sent for the Lord Jesus (see John 12).

We are told she is a widow woman. It seems that she had no one to help her emotionally, physically, mentally, spiritually or financially. She had nothing and no one except bystanders. She may have been accompanied by many people from her city, but she was completely alone till she met Christ. She was bereft of hope and broken hearted.

The young man is carried to the city gates. A gate is a place of access and a place of transference where we can enter in or come out from. The city gates were strategic and significant places, where leaders met, where decisions were made, deals struck and destinies shaped at the city gates. Something significant was about to happen. There was about to be a divine exchange of great power where death would be swallowed up in the resurrection life of Christ. Perhaps like the woman from Nain you have reached a similar crossroads in life? You feel alone and bereft of hope? God is about to meet you in your circumstance and resurrect your dreams.

Compassion and Weep Not!

13 And when the Lord saw her, he had compassion on her, and said unto her, Weep not.
The Lord saw the woman despite the huge crowds around her and the vast crowds around Him also. Jesus can find us in any situation. He is near to the broken hearted. He comes to lift up the downtrodden and places the lonely in families.

The Bible tells us Christ had compassion on her. It says He felt for her, He was reaching out in love to her but He despite this He gave her a very strange instruction. He told her to "weep not."

Jesus Himself wept at the grave of Lazarus yet here he was telling a broken hearted mother, a widow woman, who had lost her only child to, "Weep not." We have to know Jesus cared deeply about the woman's situation, which is why the Scriptures tell us He had compassion. **So why on earth would he tell her to "weep not"?**

Firstly, we must comprehend that she is already weeping. If she were not already weeping (and we can fully understand why) Jesus would not instruct her to stop. But we must also understand:

- "Weep not" did not mean Jesus was removing permission for her to grieve
- "Weep not" did not mean Jesus lacked compassion or did not care
- "Weep not" did not mean we cannot cry when we are mourning

- "Weep not" did not mean Jesus did not approve of her crying
- "Weep not" did not mean Jesus did not cry. He wept at Lazarus' tomb!

The pain of a mother losing her child is one of the deepest pains on earth. It is beyond words. It is a crushing death pain. It is a suffocating, all-consuming death pain and without the intervention of Christ it will swallow the woman up entirely. Yet, we also acknowledge that the loss of any loved one dear to us is a pain that it is indescribable and at times almost unbearable save for the comfort that Christ alone can bring.

A Command and an Instruction

Why then does the Lord say, "Weep not?" We have to understand that "Weep not" is both an instruction and it is also a command. The instruction reaches through her pain to her conscious mind. The command reaches deep into her spirit man and causes a spiritual reaction with the words of Christ. This is such a powerful revelation that we must grasp by the grace of God.

Two Resurrection Miracles

There were two resurrection miracles needed here. The first resurrection miracle was the resurrection emotionally of the widow woman who has lost her only son. Her weeping, her emotions and the devastating pain of her loss, the darkness, the despair, and the loneliness had taken her into a place of spiritual death. She is as emotionally dead as her son is physically dead. She feels like she has no hope. She has no one and nothing. She was lost in her pain and sorrow and grief. She was paralysed by her pain and could not move on in any capacity. Have you ever felt that way?

The reason Jesus told her to "weep not" is because these are words of resurrection power. When the Lord said to Lazarus "come forth" Heaven and earth moved in response to the words of Christ and the dead man was raised to life. Now these two words uttered by Christ to the widow woman at Nain, "*weep not*," were resurrecting hope and life in the woman, they were changing the spiritual atmosphere and they were about to change the story of a broken hearted mama and her dead son. Jesus was creating a person with faith to rise up in this moment because He was about to command the son to be raised to life. Jesus is speaking life to your dead circumstances right now. He is lifting you up and out into victory.

Now Jesus is about to do the second resurrection miracle and raise the widow woman's faith to raise her only dead son. But first He had to inject faith in her to bring her from the place of death back to life, to bring her to a place where she could hope for life to return to her son, even with a tiny grain of faith.

By Faith Arise

14 And he came and touched the bier: and they that bare him stood still. And he said, Young man, I say unto thee, Arise.

Now that Jesus had caught her attention, I believe a spark of faith was released in the woman and faith rose up in her. She saw all the crowds with Christ; she heard the voice of the Master; she experienced resurrection anointing piercing to the very core of her being, her spirit, her body and her soul and she cannot help but respond in faith. She dared to lift her head and to silence her weeping and in that magnificent moment she was lifted above her circumstances and God spoke beyond her emotions and pain and her spirit was activated in faith. She made a choice to focus beyond her circumstances, she listened to the voice of God, she focused on "weep not" thinking there must be a reason the Master was giving this instruction. She obeyed and the words of Christ catapulted both her and her son from death to life.

Beloved woman of God I dare you to believe in His resurrection power. I dare you to trust Him with even a grain of faith. The seemingly impossible shall become possible for those who believe in Jesus' lovely name.

Now Jesus does two things. Firstly, He touched the bier (coffin) and secondly, He spoke to the young man and wondrously he responded and was raised from death to life. The word, "Arise" is now reverberating in the mother and her faith became a catalyst for her son to be raised up to life. I love the personal interaction of Christ with people throughout His ministry. It is our model as believers to do likewise.

15 And he that was dead sat up, and began to speak. And he delivered him to his mother.

Jesus made sure the young man was delivered to his mama. The young man who was dead and buried in a coffin was now sitting up and speaking words. Can you imagine for just a second the shift in the atmosphere around this woman and her son and all those who had come to Nain and all those who were previously mourning in Nain! Wow! It was a jaw-dropping, devil-defeating, God-glorifying, dead-raising moment of explosive joy and faith!

It is my prayer that whatever circumstances you may be facing today that right now such faith and joy are imparted to you and through you for the glory of God and the transforming of the impossible.

Revival in the Region

16 And there came a fear on all: and they glorified God, saying, That a great prophet is risen up among us; and, That God hath visited his people. 17 And this rumour of him went forth throughout all Judaea, and throughout all the region round about.

The fear of God fell on the people and ascribing glory to Jesus they recognised that God had visited His people. They called Jesus a great prophet and the news about Him spread all over. The glorious testimonies went out and spread round the entire region about Jesus because of this double miracle. It is my firm conviction that revival came to all those areas that received this ministration of Christ.

We can only see *two* miracles when we understand that the first was in healing the emotions and raising the faith of the mother, who was all but spiritually dead when she met Christ. The second miracle, we understand clearly as the raising of her son at Nain from physical death back to life.

The love of God in Christ can raise the dead, bring healing and mend any and all broken hearts and revive them to life in abundance.   Apostle Jesus raised the woman's faith to resurrection level by helping her to move beyond her emotions and step into a spiritual faith response to her most awful circumstances. Today may you also experience a faith upgrade in Jesus' mighty name! I speak life in Christ to every dead situation and command resurrection grace and glory to abound to you in the name of Jesus. Amen.

CHAPTER 6 - THE REVIVALIST

TABITHA

36 Now there was at Joppa a certain disciple named Tabitha, which by interpretation is called Dorcas: this woman was full of good works and almsdeeds which she did.
37 And it came to pass in those days, that she was sick, and died: whom when they had washed, they laid her in an upper chamber.
Acts 9

Who was Tabitha?

Saint Luke skilfully weaves miracle upon miracle into the unfolding of the book of Acts as the New Testament church finds its feet, and walks by faith in the days and weeks and months following Pentecost and the great outpouring of the Spirit.

He uncovers a pearl of great price in the story of Tabitha (otherwise also known as Dorcas). Tabitha's life speaks to us on a number of different levels from discipleship to community builder, from a dead woman to a sign and a wonder. We cannot fail to be impacted and positively influenced by her life, her works and her testimony. God is looking to raise up a movement of women community builders like Tabitha throughout the world.

A Disciple

We are given few clues concerning Tabitha's background, but we can unpack quite a bit with a little careful thought. The first thing St Luke tells us about Tabitha is that she was a disciple. Before we know her in any other capacity, she is introduced to us as "*a certain **disciple** named Tabitha.*" All else that we learn about this woman is established and built upon the foundation of her identity as a daughter of the living God. As women of God this is also our precedent and primary foundation: we are His disciples.

We will learn Tabitha was many things to many people, but the most important of them all is that she was a born-again believer. She was a disciple. She was active in her faith. This fact cannot and ought not to be lost in the minutiae of details of her life being unfolded. It was the single most significant factor of her life and it was because she was a disciple that God could bring her back from death to life everlasting and in the process bring revival to the shoreline and surrounding areas of Joppa.

What Was Happening in the Area?

Saul had recently been converted and was preaching powerfully in Jerusalem to such a profound and impactful extent that there were immediate death threats against his life. He had to flee and escaped by being let down in a basket over the city wall by some of his disciples. But despite the persecution, Jerusalem was on fire with the word of God and the moving of the Holy Spirit. The church was being persecuted but the flames of revival were burning strong in the hearts of believers in the city and in the surrounding towns and villages up and down Israel including the coast line. The people of God were willing to pay any price to preach the Gospel of the Kingdom.

The Healing of Aeneas

The power of God was sweeping from Jerusalem out towards the coastal areas. Apostle Peter was passing through various quarters and came down to the saints which were living in Lydda. It was here that he found a certain man named Aeneas, who had been bed-ridden for eight years because of palsy. Peter, full of the Spirit of God, wasted no time in commanding the man to be well. *34 And Peter said unto him, Aeneas, Jesus Christ maketh thee whole: arise, and make thy bed. And he arose immediately. ³⁵ And all that dwelt at Lydda and Saron saw him, and turned to the Lord.*

The news of the miracle healing impacted all the people living in Lydda and Sharon and when they saw how the man was whole and cured, many of them turned to the Lord and were saved. The revival was spreading like wild fire as it moved towards the shoreline, edging ever nearer to Lydda where we will meet Tabitha. As we have already established, Tabitha was a disciple of the Lord Jesus Christ. She was probably part of a small community of believers in the sea shore town of Joppa. Tabitha will soon become known to us as a New Testament revivalist. Revival fires were burning and moving ever nearer.

Good Works and Alms-Giving

Tabitha's name is derived from an Aramaic word meaning 'gazelle' and speaks to us of spiritual grace and beauty. Aside from the significant fact that she is a disciple, we are told that *this woman was full of good works and almsdeeds which she did.*

Tabitha was a woman who abounded in good deeds and works of mercy and was in a position to give alms to the needy. Alms were charitable donations of money, goods, services or food given to the poor and needy. The concept of alms is incorporated in the Old Testament, when God gave instructions that fields were not to be harvested to the very edges nor was every grape in a vineyard to be lifted up. Instead they were to be left for the poor and needy (Leviticus 19:9-10). Also during every seventh year the entire field, vineyard or olive yard was to be left to rest and the poor of the land were to be permitted to take from it. (See Exodus 23:10-11)

In addition to Tabitha's alms giving, the New Testament gives us further examples. These include the gentile Cornelius, whose faithful giving of alms brought him to the Lord's attention. Subsequent to this Peter was sent to him for the purposes of sharing the Gospel. Additionally, the Greek churches sending support to the church in Jerusalem might also be considered a type of alms giving. (See Acts 24:17)

Jesus taught about alms, that our giving is not be about gaining attention for ourselves, but rather it is to be an act of worship to God. (See Matthew 6)

The Bible does not restrict alms to merely giving money. In Luke 11:41 Jesus address the Pharisees and confronts them by saying although they appear to be acting in all the right ways, they don't give alms with the right heart. They might give money to the poor, but they are bereft of mercy and love, respect or kindness for the very people they are giving to.

Peter when confronted by the lame man at the Gate Beautiful did not offer the man money but rather said, *6 Then Peter said, Silver and gold have I none; but such as I have give I thee: In the name of Jesus Christ of Nazareth rise up and walk.*

Returning to Tabitha - to be able to give to the poor it is logical to assume that Tabitha was a woman of some means. She had wealth and she had influence. We might describe her as a community builder. Tabitha is not a poor woman. She is a woman with financial capacity that makes investment in the lives of people around her. God still uses women of financial means today to advance His kingdom.

Tabitha is Dead!

To all intents and purposes Tabitha had a busy and fruitful life. She was making a difference in multiple ways but the next thing we read concerning her life is an absolute bombshell! The bible says, *37 And it came to pass in those days, that she was sick, and died: whom when they had washed, they laid her in an upper chamber. 38 And forasmuch as Lydda was nigh to Joppa, and the disciples had heard that Peter was there, they sent unto him two men, desiring him that he would not delay to come to them.*

The woman who was so full of vibrancy and life was suddenly and confusingly pronounced dead! Her life had been a beacon of light to so many, but now it was snuffed out without warning and so suddenly. There seemed to be little rhyme or reason to this devastating occurrence at this point. But time will tell us a different tale and we will ultimately marvel at the goodness of God in all. For now we ponder our unanswered questions, even if we wait impatiently for their resolution. The life of a believer is not without questions or waiting. The key to victory is to trust in God's goodness no matter what. He can see the long term plan even when we cannot see the proverbial wood for the trees.

It is heart-warming to see how the community responded to Tabitha's death. No doubt news had already reached Joppa of the miracle healing of Aeneas and that Apostle Peter was still in the area. I love the faith of that small community of believers that they send two men to go and fetch Peter to come and pray for Tabitha. They rushed to find the man of God. Even though Tabitha was quite dead, the faith of those who sent for Peter was never more alive. They believed for divine intervention and nothing short of a resurrection miracle would suffice for their beloved Tabitha. The corporate faith of believers is of great importance to God, acting as a catalyst for a great outpouring of answered prayer.

Peter wasted no time in going with them. *39 Then Peter arose and went with them. When he was come, they brought him into the upper chamber: and all the widows stood by him weeping, and shewing the coats and garments which Dorcas made, while she was with them.*

Seamstress, Entrepreneur, Business Woman

Tabitha had been laid in an upper room of sorts and was surrounded by widow women weeping. When Apostle Peter arrived they ushered him upstairs and showed him the coats and garments which Dorcas had made while she was with them. This brief line of Scripture paints a great vista of entrepreneurialism in regards to Tabitha. The widows were women in the community who had learned how to sew under the direction of Tabitha. She had used her skills as a seamstress to make the coats and garments and in so doing, had most likely also taught them how to sew. As a woman Tabitha used her gifting and influence to empower others. I am certain there are many more like Tabitha on the earth today who are ready and able to empower others to be all they can be.

Teacher, Mentor, Marketplace Mother

We have already noted that Tabitha gave alms to the poor and needy and some of those were donations but here we see another facet to her ministry in community – she empowered others with practical gifting so that they could become financially independent. Tabitha was a teacher and a community builder. Her ministry was a practical ministry that operated in the marketplace of Lydda. She equipped others helping them to achieve dignity and learning a practical skill. Not everyone's pulpit is in church. This is important for us to understand as a Kingdom principle. The Kingdom of God must affect every sphere of society.

Tabitha was a Kingdom woman with a life that shouted "transformation" from the roof tops to the dusty streets of Joppa! God had used Tabitha to shape the culture in which she was planted. Not everyone's ministry is preaching with words, or teaching the bible with verse. So many believers are empowered to be God's spokespeople in many other spheres of society.

I adore the fact that Tabitha was a woman in a male-dominated culture making a difference for God as a disciple of the Lord Jesus Christ. Like her, we too can make a huge difference just by doing one small thing with love. Tabitha was not restrained by her gender or by her marital status. Likewise, we must also walk in the same level of freedom as we seek to pursue God's best in and through our lives.

Single and Significant

What makes Tabitha's story even more striking is that she was a single woman. We do not know her age so we do not know if she was young, middle aged or old. She was likely middle aged, but that is a guesstimate. We only know she was single. We do not know if she was a widow herself or if she simply had not yet married, either way she was alone. There were no family members or husband recorded as being part of the group of mourners, only the widows were initially mentioned in the upper room where she was laid.

That aside we do read of two men who rushed to Lydda seeking the assistance of Peter on behalf of their precious dead sister in the Lord. In this we see that Tabitha *was not* isolated from the male population. Their going on her behalf speaks volumes of their esteem of Tabitha and the fellowship they had once shared. They were a community of believers not bound by the traditions of men, but walking in mutual respect and honour towards each other.

The Resurrection

40 But Peter put them all forth, and kneeled down, and prayed; and turning him to the body said, Tabitha, arise. And she opened her eyes: and when she saw Peter, she sat up. 41 And he gave her his hand, and lifted her up, and when he had called the saints and widows, presented her alive.

The crowds gave way to the quiet prayers of the now gentle giant of faith Apostle Peter. Perhaps Peter remembered the time when Jesus had taken him, and James and John to the home of Jairus, whose twelve year old daughter Jesus insisted was only "sleeping," although she had actually passed away just prior to their coming. There Peter had witnessed his Lord and Saviour lift the child by the hand from death to life. With those memories likely uppermost in his mind and with great tenderness Peter knelt before Tabitha's inert body and spoke two simple words, "*Tabitha, Arise.*"

The glory of Heaven cascaded down to earth and Tabitha arose from death to resurrection life. He took her by the hand and lifted her up. We can barely conceive of the joy in the moments that would follow.

Peter presented Tabitha to, "*the saints _and_ widows*." In this we see that Tabitha was loved by many – those who had a faith and those of none. It is this small portion of Scripture that assists us in understanding her impact went way beyond the walls of any church building.

Tabitha's life work was in the people she served by loving and equipping them day in and day out in community.

She was not described in any way as a preacher of the word of God. But it is now in her resurrection testimony that we can see the eloquence of Heaven speaking through her life. We had previously asked ourselves why did God allow His servant to die? It seemed not to make any sense but now we can see how God used tragedy to birth revival. She was God's woman. She was in the right place at the right time and wait for it … God permitted her to die…. So that He could raise her to life and impact even more lives with her remarkable story!

He used her story to become His story and truly that is how history is made: the God of Creation writes His love letter in and through our lives so that others can enter into the same relationship with Him that we are blessed to enjoy.

The Revivalist

The story finalises with news of revival reaching far and wide. *42 And it was known throughout all Joppa; and many believed in the Lord. 43 And it came to pass, that he tarried many days in Joppa with one Simon a tanner.*

Although Tabitha had lived a significant life up until the point when she had died, her resurrection testimony caused explosive and exponential increase. In every way her effectiveness as a disciple, a business woman and a community builder increased. She emerged from the ashes of the death to life experience to become a powerful revivalist. As a woman of faith, her story so powerfully speaks to us as a global company of women of faith today.

Everywhere her story was told the people believed in the Lord. And today as her story is told people all over the world can still experience the power and grace and love of God. Ruth had to pass through famine in order to find her husband Boaz and Tabitha had to pass through this great trial in order to become even more blessed and effective as a daughter of God with a fruitful ministry.

Tabitha is truly an inspirational woman revivalist of the New Testament. She did not have a husband by her side. She was not married. She was a woman in ministry, a single female disciple serving God in her community. For those with husbands in ministry it is a great joy and we thank God for marriage and for children. Let us also rejoice in how God could and still does single women for his glory.

Life-Changing

I shared Tabitha's life message when I was speaking at a women's' conference in Ireland a couple of years ago. The effect was quite astonishing. In truth I didn't expect it. The women were so impacted and for some of them it was truly life-changing. Some of the older women who had previously thought they were of no use to God suddenly realised that God could use them regardless of whether they were young, middle aged or more senior.
A number of the practically gifted women (one was a seamstress just like Tabitha) and other business women had not realised that what they did in their communities and places of work could be seen as legitimate ministry. Prior to my coming they had thought that only preaching and teaching was to be considered a viable Kingdom expression. How they rejoiced knowing that the skills and experience they had could be used by God to share the Gospel!

One lady who was a single woman finally saw that even though she was not married, God did and still does use women in ministry, whether they are married or not, a woman who loves and serves Jesus can have a fruitful and influential ministry!

It is my hope and my prayer that by sharing Tabitha's story many women the world over will be emancipated from the lie that if they are single, or older or in business, or more practically skilled than preaching orientated that they cannot or do not have a ministry.

I decree and declare in the name of Jesus Christ than ANY woman disciple of the Lord Jesus Christ whether single or married, can and does have a bona fide ministry in some respect or another. Amen

CHAPTER 7 – THE MILITARY LEADER AND JUDGE

DEBORAH

⁴ And Deborah, a prophetess, the wife of Lapidoth, she judged Israel at that time.
Judges 4

When Israel had repented of her sins the Lord raised up Ehud as a deliverer of the nation. Ehud was a Benjamite and through him God released the Hebrew people from the bondage of rulership under the Moabite king Eglon. Ehud slew king Eglon by thrusting a dagger into his belly. In fact, the king of Moab was so overweight that the dagger was not able to be withdrawn after it entered his stomach. Under Ehud's leadership the land of Israel enjoyed rest for eighty years.

After Ehud came Shamgar the son of Anath leading us to the time of Israel again doing evil in the sight of the Lord after Ehud had died. The Lord permitted Jabin the king of Canaan to oppress the people of Israel, along with his army captain Sisera. The people of Israel cried again to the Lord because of the serious nature of the military might of the Canaanite king and his army who *"mightily oppressed the children of Israel."* (Judges 4:3)

It is into this chaotic dispensation of time in the history of the people of Israel that God raised up a deliverer in the form of a woman named Deborah.

Who Is Deborah?

⁴ And Deborah, a prophetess, the wife of Lapidoth, she judged Israel at that time. ⁵ And she dwelt under the palm tree of Deborah between Ramah and Bethel in mount Ephraim: and the children of Israel came up to her for judgment.

Deborah is introduced to us being described in her multi-faceted aspects of functionality and relationship. We will later learn of her military prowess but the initial verses do not yet address her role in the strategic military exercise that saved her nation. What then can we gauge from our first encounter with this remarkable woman of God?

Deborah – "Queen Bee"

The name Deborah means *bee*, and comes from the Hebrew root meaning *to speak or to pronounce with intelligence.* She was, indeed, an intelligent woman with capacity for speech in the realm of prophecy, council, judging the nation, military leadership and much more! Perhaps she was more akin to a Queen bee!

Women of God we have a role model of great significance in Deborah. We too can speak intelligently and strategically at many levels. Be encouraged. Find your voice and speak with humility and holy boldness when instructed by God to do so. Remember that silence also has its place. Jesus Himself uttered not a word when he could have defended Himself. Wisdom is in the balance of knowing when to be silent and knowing when to speak.

A Prophetess

The second thing we are told about Deborah is that she was a prophetess. From this we may confidently assert that she was a God-fearing woman who loved the Lord. She had a close relationship with God and was able to receive revelation and wisdom from the Lord. She gave counsel to others both with respect to her wisdom and also in regards to her significant prophetic revelatory gifting.

Too often we major on the fact that the bible narrates that Queen Jezebel was a woman who operated in a counterfeit anointing. We wax lyrical on all her short comings and her evil intent. She was, indeed, an evil queen and a counterfeit prophetess. But I like that in the life of Deborah we see the clear and shining example of a Godly woman prophetess, who led in the nation of Israel with great integrity and authority. May we give more attention to Deborah's virtue than to that of a defeated Jezebel, whilst at the same time ensuring our lives are free from any such snare.

Deliverer of a Nation - A Woman

We are told that Deborah is the wife of Lapidoth and that she judged Israel at that time. "*That time*" is the time of civil unrest, great fear and disruption under the rule of the Canaanite king Jabin and his heinous war captain Sisera. It was most certainly not an easy time for any person to rule, and yet, Deborah a woman, was in the position of being one of the key leaders and voices in the nation that people trusted and responded to. Her example to us is without question, of meteoric proportions. She is aspirational.

Her Position in the Nation was Not Determined by Her Marital Status

It is interesting to note that whilst Deborah was married, her position and influence in the nation are not because of her marital status. The Scriptures tell us nothing about her husband Lapidoth, only that Deborah is his wife. We might assume that they were happily married and that they were a good team. What blesses me is that Deborah did not rely on her husband's status in order to be functional in the Kingdom of God. They were most assuredly husband and wife and they each had a role to play. What Lapidoth's role was is not made clear in the Scriptures except that we might assume he was a wonderful husband, loving, faithful and totally supportive of his wife in her essential roles as a national deliverer. We thank God for the blessing of marriage yet Deborah was not a powerful national leader because of her husband. She was a powerful national leader because she loved and served God.

Judge and Governmental Leader

Deborah judged Israel at that time. We learn that in her role as a Judge in Israel that the children of Israel would come up to her for judgement. They would bring all of their issues and problems to her and she would give judicial input. Her wise decisions and counsel were invaluable. She was a much sought after governmental and strategic leader in the nation of Israel. We cannot underplay the significance of Deborah's national leadership role. God is rising up Deborah's in the earth today. Godly women belong and have significant input to make at strategic level meetings and in the highest echelons of society.

Military Strategist

Having been briefly introduced to Deborah, we are now given further insight into her ever-expanding role in Israel. We are about to meet *Deborah the Military Strategist!*

⁶ And she sent and called Barak the son of Abinoam out of Kedeshnaphtali, and said unto him, Hath not the LORD God of Israel commanded, saying, Go and draw toward mount Tabor, and take with thee ten thousand men of the children of Naphtali and of the children of Zebulun? ⁷ And I will draw unto thee to the river Kishon Sisera, the captain of Jabin's army, with his chariots and his multitude; and I will deliver him into thine hand. ⁸ And Barak said unto her, If thou wilt go with me, then I will go: but if thou wilt not go with me, then I will not go. ⁹ And she said, I will surely go with thee: notwithstanding the journey that thou takest shall not be for thine honour; for the LORD shall sell Sisera into the hand of a woman. And Deborah arose, and went with Barak to Kedesh. ¹⁰ And Barak called Zebulun and Naphtali to Kedesh; and he went up with ten thousand men at his feet: and Deborah went up with him.

Deborah called for Barak, meaning she called (commanded) him to come and meet with her where she held court. Barak was the Israeli equivalent to Sisera the army commander in the camp of the enemy. Barak was the much respected commander of the armies of Israel.

Deborah had evidently received some kind of prophetic direction from God as she called for Barak and said to him, *Hath not the LORD God of Israel commanded, saying, Go and draw toward mount Tabor, and take with thee ten thousand men of the children of Naphtali and of the children of Zebulun?*

Deborah was not speaking out of her own opinion, but was speaking out of the authority of both her respected position as a Judge in Israel and also in the authority of the prophetic revelatory command she had received from God. She was to make known to Barak the will of God to go towards Mount Tabor and take 10,000 troops with him from the tribes of Naphtali and Zebulun. She prophesied that God was going to lure Sisera, the captain of king Jabin's army to the river Kishon and that there God would deliver the multitudes into his hand. In her sphere of influence Deborah's authority was equal to that of Barak.

Barak's Response

Barak's response to Deborah's command and to her prophetic directive is worth some analysis. Scrutinising his words reveals a great deal more than we initially may comprehend. Barak states that he will only go to war against Sisera if Deborah goes with him. He goes so far as to say that if she doesn't go with him he isn't willing to go at all! Many have construed Barak's words to be lacking in courage but this is not at all how I interpret his reaction.

Firstly, when Deborah called for Barak to her court he came without hesitation. This tells us that Barak esteemed Deborah in her role of Judge in the nation. He had the utmost respect for her authority as a national leader and hence answered her request to enter her court. It is logical to assume there was a mutual respect between Deborah and Barak as Godly leaders; since Deborah acted without question upon the prophetic revelation she had received from the Lord and called Barak into her court without hesitation. She did not question God's choice.

Secondly, after Deborah had spoken (prophetically) to Barak about going to battle against Sisera, he did not refute the authenticity or legitimacy of the prophecy concerning the downfall of Sisera. Barak did not deny the prophetic revelatory validity, interpretation or accuracy of what Deborah had spoken to him. This reveals that Barak also respected and honoured the prophetic grace upon Deborah's life. I do not believe he was in doubt with regard to the word of the Lord.

Plurality and Honour not Gender Bias

What then should be our understanding of Barak's refusal to go into battle without Deborah? I propose it is about a reciprocal appreciation and plurality concerning each other's leadership roles in the nation of Israel at that time.

Some suggest that Barak's initial hesitation is about Deborah somehow being stronger than he. I don't view it that way at all. In reality I think that gender is not an issue at all in the lives of Deborah and Barak, in truth I regard it as quite the reverse.

Deborah at no point is described as physically wielding a weapon. That role is reserved for the military might and prowess of Barak and his armies. Deborah is the strategic military leader that comes alongside of the powerful military expertise of Barak to see an enemy defeated under the headship of God Almighty himself. They are operating in their God-given authority and NOT in their gender identities! How wonderful to see an anointed man and woman of God operating in their God-given authority – not in competition with each other but working in total collaboration with the plans of God.

Deborah says she will go with Barak but then explained that Sisera will be given into the hands of a woman. It is important to note that the unnamed woman could not fulfil her role without Barak first fulfilling his. He lead the armies along with the strategic military input of Deborah and through this joint military manoeuvre, another woman was then positioned in the purposes of God to do the part she had been pre-ordained to do. Barak proceeded to call the tribes of Zebulun and Naphtali to Kedesh and there he went up with 10,000 men and Deborah was with them.

14 And Deborah said unto Barak, Up; for this is the day in which the LORD hath delivered Sisera into thine hand: is not the LORD gone out before thee? So Barak went down from mount Tabor, and ten thousand men after him. 15 And the LORD discomfited Sisera, and all his chariots, and all his host, with the edge of the sword before Barak; so that Sisera lighted down off his chariot, and fled away on his feet.

Aware of the Israeli troops amassing against him, Sisera gathered 900 of his chariots and innumerable troops and the battle lines were drawn. Deborah spoke powerfully to Barak again, this time she instructed him to go down from Mount Tabor to meet the advancing enemy army under Sisera. One might wonder how a military captain would take on such advice!

The vantage point in warfare is always from the high place, but here was a female leader telling a male leader to go down from his vantage point and engage the enemy at a low level. One again we see the brilliance of Godly honour between this man and woman of God. Deborah did not doubt the strategy God gave her and neither did Barak. Both acted in obedience and in a timely fashion to the word of the Lord and it brought them absolute success in the battle. Barak took down every last man of the enemy army with the exception of Sisera who fled away into the tent of Jael, the wife of Heber the Kenite (because there was peace between Jabin king of Hazor and the house of Heber the Kenite). Jael went out to meet Sisera.

Jael and the Hammer of the Lord

17 Howbeit Sisera fled away on his feet to the tent of Jael the wife of Heber the Kenite: for there was peace between Jabin the king of Hazor and the house of Heber the Kenite. 18 And Jael went out to meet Sisera, and said unto him, Turn in, my lord, turn in to me; fear not. And when he had turned in unto her into the tent, she covered him with a mantle. 19 And he said unto her, Give me, I pray thee, a little water to drink; for I am thirsty. And she opened a bottle of milk, and gave him drink, and covered him. 20 Again he said unto her, Stand in the door of the tent, and it shall be, when any man doth come and enquire of thee, and say, Is there any man here? that thou shalt say, No.

It was traditional for the wife of the host to greet the approaching guest. It was part of the culture and custom of Jael's people. It was a role of honour to go and offer hospitality to a guest or friend seeking sanctuary. Jael was fulfilling her people's customs as she met and welcomed Sisera.

A friend entering into the tent was tantamount to what we might describe today as "political asylum." It was an automatic rule of thumb that the person entering the tent to seek hospitality and refuge would be protected from any pursuant enemy and any ensuing external attackers. Sisera, therefore, considered himself to be in a safe place of the tent with Jael.

It is at this point that we must marvel afresh at the way in which God used an "unknown" woman to finalise His plans for deliverance of the nation of Israel from the evil king Jabin and his equally wicked army captain Sisera.

Jael had no earthly reason to betray her husband or her people and do what she did next: which was to drive a tent peg firmly and in a deadly fashion into the temples of Sisera as he slept on the ground inside the tent! In reality she had every reason NOT to do such a thing.

She was breaking cultural rules of hospitality; her people's rules of tradition; the unspoken rules of sanctuary; she was flying in the opposite direction of her husband's wishes but somehow this quiet woman received the mind of God and executed His will. Please let us be wise and state that we are not advocating women rush to pick up hammers and nails. Not at all! The only option left to God was to take out Sisera and the least collateral damage was for that to be done at the hands of Jael. Sisera was a casualty of war that could not be avoided if God was to deliver an entire nation back to freedom and peace. This is the context in which we must view the death of Sisera.

Jael exited her tent to be met by Barak who was in pursuit of Sisera and she told him, *"Come, and I will show thee the man whom thou seekest. And when he came into her tent, behold, Sisera lay dead, and the nail was in his temples. v22b*

God subdued His enemies that day and as a result the children of Israel prospered and prevailed against Jabin the king of Canaan until he was destroyed.

A Poet and a Singer

5 *Then sang Deborah and Barak the son of Abinoam on that day, saying,* **2** *Praise ye the LORD for the avenging of Israel, when the people willingly offered themselves.* **3** *Hear, O ye kings; give ear, O ye princes; I, even I, will sing unto the LORD; I will sing praise to the LORD God of Israel.*

After the death of Sisera, the Biblical narrative takes an interesting turn to reveal yet another aspect to Deborah. She and Barak sang a song of victory unto the Lord. In the heat of warfare and now in the aftermath of peace in the nation, Deborah and Barak remain united in the purposes of God, as one with the mind of the Lord.

Not only was she a prophetess, a judge and a military leader, Deborah was also an accomplished poet and a singer!

Deborah had a wonderfully creative aspect to her personality as well as being a gifted governmental leader.

Role Model

Deborah was a mobiliser in her nation. She had the capacity to gather for Kingdom purposes. She accessed the mind of God through wisdom and by revelation. She trusted God and believed in Him when others doubted. She had incredible faith and walked with God through some tortuously difficult times with her people. She was respected as a leader in various capacities and she emerges as a brilliant military strategist in partnership with Barak the military commander of the armies of Israel. Deborah appeared to live a life without fear, control or limitation because she walked in obedience to the will of God. She cared for people and was willing to risk her own life for the sake of others.

She had favour with political leaders, tribal leaders and royalty as well as favour with the ordinary men and women in the streets of Israel at that time. She was courageous in times of peace and equally intrepid in times of warfare. She led without compromise as a woman of Godly integrity and she led from the front.

She was a defender of righteousness and a devout woman of God. She believed in the strength of God more than she believed in the strength of a king. She walked in radical obedience and was an example to all around her. She was willing to pay a price to walk with God and she risked her life to save the lives of multitudes.

She was a team player and knew how to walk with other great leaders in humility and holy boldness. May many more Deborah's arise in our day in strategic and blessed roles in the nations!

A Mother in Israel

7 The inhabitants of the villages ceased, they ceased in Israel, until that I Deborah arose, that I arose a mother in Israel.

Deborah is described as a mother in Israel. There is nothing in Scripture to indicate that this is about physical motherhood. Although we know she was married to Lapidoth, there is nothing in the text or history books that suggest Deborah had any physical natural children of her own. What then is this phenomenon of being *a mother in Israel* if it does not relate to physically bearing children?

19 I am one of them that are peaceable and faithful in Israel: thou seekest to destroy a city and a mother in Israel: why wilt thou swallow up the inheritance of the LORD? 20 And Joab answered and said, Far be it, far be it from me, that I should swallow up or destroy. 2 Samuel

The phrase "*mother in Israel*" is attributed to another woman (whom Scripture does not name), in 2 Samuel 20 whom Good uses in a strategic military discussion with Joab the commander of the armies of Israel under the rule of King David. As a result of the rebellion of Sheba and his taking refuge in the city of Abel of Beth Maachan, Joab and his men had surrounded the city. Joab was about to sack the city and leave no living soul under the orders of king David. However, he met this woman and through her wisdom and strategic intervention in her dialogue he spared the city. She persuaded Joab to take only the rebel Sheba and to spare the city. She was able to identify the traitor and his head was thrown over the city wall to Joab. Joab then blew the trumpet and returned to King David in Jerusalem. This woman is also referred to as *a mother in Israel*.

It would behove us to consider that *a mother in Israel* is a person whom God raises up to defend and deliver His people at a time of national crisis. In the two cases before us of Deborah and the unnamed woman of 2 Samuel, these individuals happen to be women. However, their being named as *a mother in Israel* is not as a result of their physical giving birth. It is as a result of their functionality of being used in God's hands as national deliverers. Firstly for the people of Israel and secondly, for other nations.

They are true heroines of the faith; not that women who are mothers are any less heroines of the faith! We see in the lives of the matriarchs Sarah, Rebecca and Rachel the most tremendous value in being biological mothers who give birth to sons who become fathers of the faith and are great kingdom giants.

However, let us not play down the role of motherhood to only being an "incubator" through whom kings are birthed to rise up to bring glory to God. Women as well as men have essential strategic national roles to play in God's plans in their many and varied roles and functionalities both in church and in society.

CHAPTER 8 - THE SENT WOMAN

MARY MAGDALENE

11But Mary stood without at the sepulchre weeping: and as she wept, she stooped down, and looked into the sepulchre,
John 20

Who is Mary?

Before Mary (of Magda) met Jesus her life didn't make much sense. She was a former demoniac, bound up by sin, a social outcast and one who had lived in hopelessness and despair. Jesus Himself delivered her from the seven demons that had tormented her. With a grateful heart she became His disciple and a loyal Christ-follower who was involved in ministry with Him and along with other women she financially supported the Lord's ministry too.

Daily she was a witness to His many miracles and acts of selfless love. Jesus gave Mary's life meaning. She adored Him. When she was with Him, her life had purpose and focus. Jesus was her everything.

Mary was there at the end when she, along with just a handful of others near the cross, watched as He was crucified. She was faithful to the end. She could not bear to watch the torture and torment He endured and yet she could not bear to leave Him whilst still a beat of His glorious heart whispered life.

She saw her Master's last breath drain from Him and she heard Him whisper the eternal words, *"It is finished"*. Her heart was torn apart with the pain of separation from her Beloved. She had grown so close to Christ and His parting was too much for her to bear. She could not comprehend His going.

He had emptied himself out in love on the Cross and now Mary was in anguish. She too was empty. How could life be lived without His daily presence, or the wonder of His smile and the warmth of His friendship?

Mary's Condition

Mary was broken-hearted and bereft of hope. She cried for two days and two nights, until her eyes were red and raw. She barely slept. The weight of loss consumed her. She could not bear the thought of living out her tomorrows without Christ. It was too painful to contemplate. Yet somehow despite her sorrow, resolve rose up from the depths of Mary's being and she made her way to the tomb where her Passion lay.

It was early in the morning. Sleep had eluded her and as dawn broke the emotions were strong and almost unbearable. She dragged herself along with the weight of sorrow and sought to anoint her Lord with spices. Each step was agony. What would she find? Her mind was filled with blood-stained images of the brutality He had endured. His face torn and blooded, His beautiful head pierced with a cruel crown of thorns. She remembered His silent screams as bone lashed at His bone and ripped Him apart with each beating. She recalled His bruised and aching flesh and the vicious nails, which had pierced His hands and feet. And she remembered the spear that had pierced His side and the blood and water that flowed. Despite her anguish each step took her closer to the only One who could heal her pain. Tomorrow was too painful without Him. She sought Him with all her heart.

The Stone Rolled Away!

Mary was not prepared for what she found. The stone was rolled away! Her Master's body had been taken! Terror and confusion engulfed her. Where was He? Who had taken her beloved? She ran to find Simon Peter and the other disciple, saying, *2 Then she runneth, and cometh to Simon Peter, and to the other disciple, whom Jesus loved, and saith unto them,*

They have taken away the Lord out of the sepulchre, and we know not where they have laid him. John 20

Responding to Mary's cry, the others ran ahead to the tomb. They found the tomb empty as Mary had said, with strips of linen lying along with the burial cloth that had been around Jesus' head. Eventually the others left the tomb, but Mary stood outside and wept. After everyone else had gone, Mary could not bear to depart. She was fearful and trembling but earnestly she sought her King. A fresh well of tears burst from her eyes as she sought Christ.

In humility she bent over into the tomb and saw two angels in white, seated where Jesus body had been. The angels asked her why she was crying. She replied, [13] *And they say unto her, Woman, why weepest thou? She saith unto them, Because they have taken away my Lord, and I know not where they have laid him.* The angels were magnificent but Mary barely noticed them. Her only concern was to find Christ. At this, she turned round and saw Jesus standing there but she did not realise that it was He. [15]*Jesus saith unto her, Woman, why weepest thou? whom seekest thou?* Thinking He was the gardener, she said, *"Sir, if thou have borne him hence, tell me where thou hast laid him, and I will take him away.*

Mary had mistaken Jesus for the gardener. Her grief consumed her and momentarily she had forgotten to seek Christ amongst the living, rather than the dead. She was desperate to find her beloved. Lovesick she thought she could carry His body all by herself. She had learned that faith laughs at impossibility and love performs the deed.

Then time stood still for Mary. He spoke her name. [16]*Jesus saith unto her, Mary. She turned herself, and saith unto him, Rabboni; which is to say, Master.*

"*Mary*" Jesus said to her. She turned towards Him and her eyes were opened. Finally, she was reunited with the desire of her heart: the One who gave her life meaning. It was true.

The stone was rolled away and He had risen! Resurrection revelation flooded through her and waves of spiritual understanding restored and revived her. Finally, Mary beheld the Resurrected Christ. When He spoke her name, her heart began to beat again to the tune of eternity and her tortured being exploded with rivers of joy. Her Jesus was alive! His Blood sacrifice on Calvary had conquered sin and death. He ever lives to bring us from death to life and to speak our names so personally.

Mary's Commission – Tell the World I am Alive!

Jesus loved and trusted Mary. She was the first one to see Him after His death on the cross. Her being found was not dependent on her own efforts. His heart knew how much she longed to be with him. He found her even as she sought Him. What joy was His to pour love upon this precious servant. But there is much more we must accede to in Jesus' commission to Mary.

17 Jesus saith unto her, Touch me not; for I am not yet ascended to my Father: but go to my brethren, and say unto them, I ascend unto my Father, and your Father; and to my God, and your God.

Mary had found favour and honour in her Master's eyes. She ran to the disciples and told them she had seen the Lord, telling them all that Jesus had instructed her. *18 Mary Magdalene came and told the disciples that she had seen the LORD, and that he had spoken these things unto her.*

Mary – An Apostle Messenger - A Sent One

Until this time women at the time of Christ being alive on the earth were not treated with much dignity by society. They were not considered to be reliable witnesses and could not even give evidence in court. Jesus commissioned Mary to go and share the most important news in history. He sent a woman to do the job that prior to His sacrifice at Calvary only a man could do. This "sending" of Mary to the apostles is apostolic and it is emancipating on a global level. Her being sent took women beyond even the glorious condition of being with God in Eden, to post-Calvary now being in Christ.

Jesus Chose A Woman Witness

Jesus intentionally, deliberately and redemptively chose Mary, a woman, to be His apostolic messenger. Don't let the weight and enormity of this blessing pass you by. Jesus restored everything. He restored everyone willing to walk in covenant with Him back to the Father. Mary of Magda was walking in a "sent one's" capacity to be a witness to and for the resurrected Christ!

Mary's name means "tower" and she certainly stood tall in that moment and remains an inspiration to both men and women today. She had overcome so much suffering, heartache and adversity to follow Christ. She emerged from the ashes of her broken past to be a history changer, a world shaper, an apostolic woman of God who had a key role both in the time of Jesus earthly ministry and in the church after He ascended to glory.

Some history books described Mary of Magda as "the apostle to the apostles." I wouldn't go this far at present in my own portrayal of Mary but it is a fascinating depiction worthy of consideration.

Precious ones seek the Risen King with all of your heart. Pursue His presence with faith and holy passion. Reach out for the Master, knowing that His arms are already extended in amazing love towards you.

Women of God, run with the message of life He has entrusted to us all. He lives, He loves, He forgives, He heals, and He delivers. He is our glory and the radiance of our Father. He is Peace and Mercy. He is Grace. He has triumphed over death and sickness and poverty. He is our Shalom and He is sending women forth in every culture in every nation on the face of the earth to carry the Good News of the Gospel –

Christ is Alive! He sends us to be His disciples and to make disciples of all nations. Women are not an after-thought; we are not "less than" in the eyes of our Heavenly Father. The Master has need of us and it our joy to serve alongside and with our brothers in the Lord until Christ returns at His second coming.

It is never easy to end a book like this when so many other inspiring and life-changing stories are waiting to be written. It is my prayer that this first volume of *God's Wonder Women* will be catalytic in birthing many into their Kingdom destiny, and most especially God's precious women all over the world.

The Hollywood block buster *Wonder Woman* took the world by storm in 2017. Now may God's wonder women emerge alongside of His precious sons to advance the Kingdom of God in every nation till Jesus returns!

Together for our King and His Kingdom,
Apostle Catherine Brown
Founder/International Director
Gatekeepers Global Ministries
https://www.facebook.com/Catherine-Brown-509043002615968/

ABOUT THE AUTHOR

Apostle Catherine Brown is the founder/director of Gatekeepers Global Ministries. She is a strategic Kingdom builder who ministers internationally working alongside individuals, churches and marketplace leaders assisting them in discipleship, strategising, training, leadership development and community transformation. She is a prolific author and has published 17 books.

Facebook: https://www.facebook.com/Catherine-Brown-509043002615968/
Twitter: CBrownGGM
Web: www.gatekeepers.org.uk;
www.transparentpublishing.co.uk
Email: Catherine@gatekepers.org.uk
Tel: 0843 289 4707
You tube: Apostle Catherine Brown

OTHER BOOKS BY THE AUTHOR

LEAH

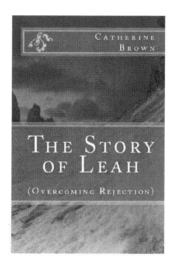

Leah's story is inspirational and her courage and tenacity in the midst of extremely difficult circumstances speak profoundly to us. She is a powerful testimony as to how a person can choose to overcome rejection and trust in God's faithfulness and grace to carry them beyond defeat, into a time of refreshing and personal renewal and restoration. In addition to Leah's story, the author has included practical notes on how to recognize rejection and how to pray for healing from its debilitating effects. (49pp)

THE INVESTED LEADER

By Catherine Brown

The Invested Leader is an invaluable Kingdom resource for all those in Christian leadership. The book will also benefit many secular leaders. The topics of mentoring, teaching, instructing, coaching, parenting, understanding fatherhood, raising sons and daughters is a timeless one with eternal value and critical global consequence in our day. It has never been more crucial in history to understand that there can be no success without a successor. Brown goes beyond popular idioms and takes the reader on an in-depth journey enabling them along the way to create a strategic response to this essential leadership paradigm. Brown has been actively involved in pastoring pastors and discipling leaders and believers for more than twenty years, throughout multiple denominations and nations. In The Invested Leader she shares practical and spiritual leadership principles that will enable church, ministry and marketplace leaders in every sphere to create an environment and an strategy for engaging, shaping and coaching an emerging generation of global leaders. Brown shares Biblical truths and deeply held values of what it means to be a leader who raises others to fulfil their God-given destiny. The books lays the foundation of the Father's heart for all families; God's succession plan to save all generations in Christ; principles of legacy and managing transition as well as taking an in-depth look at types of father figures and types of sons. By God's grace, Brown's international ministry is replete with the fruit of the message she writes about in The Invested Leader – the raising and maturing of spiritual sons and daughters with whom she works in Kingdom partnership worldwide. Don't miss this gem of a book. It's a treasure trove of wisdom will not only change your life, but the lives of all those you invest in!

"The Invested Leader is a must read for every leader. I believe that it can transform the way we do Kingdom." Apostle Wale Adefarasin

THE IMPERFECT LEADER

The Imperfect Leader is a must read for every Kingdom leader regardless of their culture, denomination, gender, experience or lack thereof. Brown skilfully and sensitively unpacks some of the pressing issues that leaders face today, offering invaluable practical wisdom and Biblical spiritual insights as she shares from more than 20 years of ministry experience in excess of 60 nations.

UNDERSTANDING THE KINGDOM OF GOD

Understanding the Kingdom of God" is a tremendous Christian discipleship resource for believers and leaders from all walks of life and in every culture. Brown unpacks the message of the Kingdom in a clear and uncomplicated manner, giving Biblical answers to pressing questions: What is the Kingdom? When does it come? How do we enter into the Kingdom? What are the signs of the Kingdom? The Kingdom of God is not some high and unattainable philosophical ideal. It is the reality of God in us, God with us, worked out in our daily lives as we walk with and for Him. Whether you are a student or a teacher of God's word, you will not fail to be encouraged, edified and educated through this Scriptural study. Your life can never remain the same as
you seek God's Kingdom!

Printed in Poland
by Amazon Fulfillment
Poland Sp. z o.o., Wrocław